# CHAIR CANING

## A PRACTICAL GUIDE TO WEAVING CANE SEATS

RACHAEL
SOUTH

# CHAIR CANING

## A PRACTICAL GUIDE TO WEAVING CANE SEATS

THE CROWOOD PRESS

# CONTENTS

CHAPTER 1

# TOOLS, MATERIALS AND PREPARATION

To begin, I'm going to outline what you will need in terms of tools and materials to cane your first chair. It is a relatively simple kit and once you have acquired the cane and a few of the tools listed, all you would need to find is a small wooden chair designed to have a woven cane panel for its seat or back. These chairs are not hard to find; characteristically it would be a simple wooden frame and all four of the seat rails would have spaced holes sized approximately 4–5mm wide drilled through them. The size of the holes and spacing can vary from chair to chair.

The chair cane can be bought from two or three specialist suppliers here in the UK. I'd really recommend using one of these stockists as they are used to sourcing the best quality cane – it would be a shame to spend all the time and effort of weaving a chair seat for it not to last due to inferior materials. If the cane isn't of good quality, it may prove harder to work with as it will split and snap.

The tool kit required for caning chairs isn't vast. As you can see from the list below, a few specialised tools are all you need to begin. You may already have similar tools at home; many chair caners use repurposed household items in their kits. One chair caner I knew just liked to use a small metal nail file with a hooked end. I keep a selection of different size blunt nails for use as hole clearers and have various handmade shell bodkins, as a range of sizes of tools is useful for the variety of hole sizes on the cane chair frame.

All the tools are items which you could find at a local hardware shop or one of the chair cane supply shops. Don't worry if you are having any trouble sourcing tools, I find that my own fingers are the most used of all the tools I have at my disposal!

## TOOLS

**Hole clearer** – for clearing the old cane and pegs from the drilled holes in the chair frame. A blunt nail would also work for this job.
**Bodkin** – a real go-to tool, useful for moving cane around and opening space to weave. Bodkins are a tool used in many industries; any small metal pointed tool would do for this job.
**Shell bodkin** – a bodkin which is slightly curved and has a valley in the centre. This is a tool specifically used by chair caners.

Cane panels and tools.

**Side cutters** – a sharp set of pliers with one flat side, for making close cuts.
**Hammer** – a light hammer is most suitable for tapping in pegs.
**Wooden mallet** – is also suitable for tapping in pegs or for use with the hole clearer.
**Golf tees; wooden, willow or plastic pegs** – for holding the cane tight while weaving. If you are making your own willow pegs, they would need to be 5–6cm long. You can whittle the willow to a suitable point or, if you are making wooden pegs, split some soft wood into strips approximately 1cm square. Then shape the ends into a point in the same way. I use a mix of wood, willow and golf tees depending on the size and depth of the holes.
**Steamer** – a smooth strap with a hole in the centre or at each end, used for the weavings stage of the caning process.
**Blunt nail** – really useful for clearing holes or tapping in the pegs.
**Pocket knife or scissors**
**Spring clamp** – for holding canes in place when close caning.
**Bowl** – for water and a towel, cloth or sponge.

## MATERIALS

The cane we use for seating is the bark of the rattan palm, also known as common rattan (*Calamus* sp. or *Daemonorops* sp.). These plant species are native to Southeast Asia. It is a jungle creeper which grows like ivy around the jungle floor, stretching up to the jungle canopy. Growing to very long lengths, up to 150 metres, it makes an ideal material for weaving.

The processing industry is focused in Indonesia, the Philippines and Malaysia. These countries have long-established rattan growing and processing industries. They are mostly small rural businesses so don't impact the environment in a negative way. After harvesting, the long rattans are cut down and hung up to dry out. They then undergo a sulphuration process to kill any fungus or insects. Next, the long thorns and leaves are removed, then it is split, and the centre of the rattan palm is removed. This part of the plant can be used to peg the holes on the chair frame once the seat is woven and is also used for basketry. The rattan palm is not hollow like bamboo; the cane we use for weaving seats is the outer bark of the plant. Once the bark is removed from the centre cane it is then

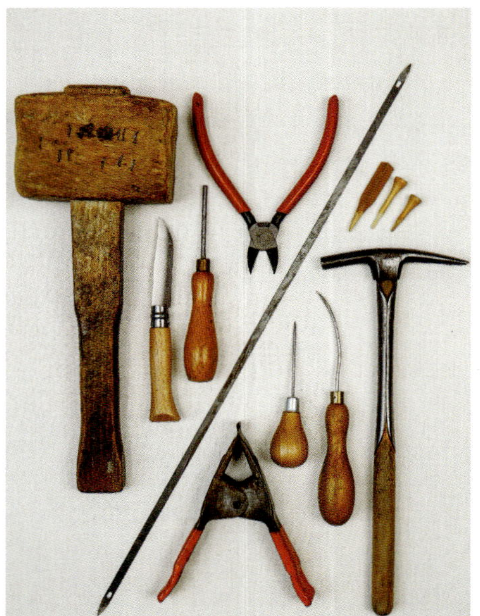

Caning tools.

Cane.

'shaved' to make ribbons of appropriate thickness and width needed for chair seating.The outer bark of the cane is a rich gold in colour, slightly rounded, smooth and shiny. The other side is fibrous and absorbent. If you look closely you will see 'nodes' on the cane – this is a part of the plant where the leaves sprout and can be a weak spot. Always use the cane with the shiny side facing upwards as it naturally repels dirt.

## Choosing Cane Size and Preparation for Use

Your cane chair will have seat rails which are usually 5–6cm wide and 1.5–2cm deep. They will have holes drilled all the way through the frame from top to bottom, on all four sides. Be aware that the spacing on holes is not always uniform! Very often the side rail holes don't line up and the distance between holes can vary widely. Don't worry, this is usual for a handmade chair and although it will affect the woven pattern, it will also add character to the restored chair.

Chair caners each have their preferred way of preparing the cane for use. I take a small bunch of cane which is looped in half, I hold the loops together with an elastic band and then coil the bunch into a bowl of water. As the cane is a plant it's absorbent, so when soaked it takes in the water, expands and becomes soft and pliable, ideal for weaving. You can remove the cane after 10–15 minutes and keep it wrapped in a damp towel. As a beginner, it is essential that your cane is soft and pliable – weaving the later stages of the pattern, it can be very frustrating if the cane snaps because it is too dry and brittle. It is handy to have a flannel, spray or sponge just to dampen the canes down, particularly if you're weaving a large area. Some caners leave the cane in the water for the whole time that they are weaving, just to make sure it is pliable enough. Others prefer to use the cane completely dry or dampen the dry canes with a sponge as they go.

If you don't use all the dampened cane at once, you can hang it up to dry ready for the next time. Just be aware that if you soak it and dry it out repeatedly, it may lose its golden colour.

| Holes Per 15cm | Cane Size | Old Cane Size |
|---|---|---|
| 16–17 | 1.5 and 1.9mm | 0 and 1 |
| 15 | 1.9 and 2.1mm | 1 and 2 |
| 14 | 1.9 and 2.1mm or all 2.1mm | 1 and 2 or all 2 |
| 13–14 | 2.1 and 2.4mm or all 2.1mm | 2 and 3 or all 2 |
| 11–12 | 2.1 and 2.4mm or all 2.4mm | 2 and 3 or all 3 |
| | Or 2.1 and 2.9mm | or 2 and 4 |
| 7–10 | 2.4 and 2.9mm | 3 and 4 |
| | 2.1 and 2.9mm or all 2.9mm | 2 and 4 or all 4 |

The cane comes in a few different sizes; the millimetre measurements refer to the width of the cane. Originally, they were simply graded by numbers 1–6 but now the cane is sold by the millimetre measurement. Many seats traditionally use a combination of two sizes for different stages of the woven pattern. Usually a thicker size is used for the diagonal weaves (crossings) and a thinner size is used for the horizontals and verticals (weavings and settings). The combination of sizes balances the overall look of the caned panel. The edge or 'beading' cane is thicker, usually around 3.9mm to 4mm. The millimetre size may vary depending on your supplier.

It is useful to keep some of the original cane panel to work out the cane sizes. If there isn't any cane on the chair, you can use the table above as a size guide.

Measure 15cm along the drilled holes in the frame. Count how many holes there are in the 15cm.

# CHAIR FRAME PREPARATION

An ideal first project would be a Victorian or Edwardian bedroom chair. These were made in great numbers and are relatively common. Very often, for want of finding a chair caner, they have a plywood board with drilled holes in a decorative pattern nailed on to the chair frame.

You can look underneath the seat for the cane holes in the seat rails to check if the chair is designed for caning.

## CLEARING THE OLD CANE

**Step 1** – To clear the old cane, use scissors to cut the caned seat out close to the frame and keep it for size, colour and pattern reference.

**Step 2** – Snip the loops on the underneath of the chair using side cutters, scissors or a pocketknife.

**Step 3** – Turn the chair back upright and then snip the beading (the wide cane edging) if the chair has it.

**Step 4** – Turn the chair back upside down and using the hole clearer and a mallet or a blunt nail and a hammer, gently tap the old cane and pegs out of the holes. Note: it is always good practice to use a wooden-handled tool (the hole clearer) with a wooden mallet or if using a metal nail, tap this with a metal hammer. The chair seat will now be clear of all the old cane and the holes should be unblocked.

Cane removed from the chair seat.

Loops cut on the underside of the chair frame.

Beading cut on the top of the chair frame.

Clearing the holes.

## CHAIR FRAME REPAIRS

If the chair has loose joints, it is useful to re-glue and clamp these to tighten them up. Gently tap the rails open and apply a little wood glue. Clamp the rails and if you have time, leave to dry overnight.

Occasionally you will see the seat rails of the chair split where the drilled holes are. The holes can create weakness in the frame, so it is common to see breaks on this part of the chair. This can be remedied using the following steps.

**Step 1** – Gently open the spilt up – you can use a small wedge of wood to hold it open. Apply some wood glue into the split.

**Step 2** – You will need some small wood screws to help the repair take the pressure of the tight cane work. These can be screwed in from the inside of the rail. Make a pilot hole with a drill first and be careful to place the screws between the weaving holes. If you don't put the screws in, it is likely the glued split will open again as the caned pattern is woven.

Split rail with glue.

Repair with screws.

## CHAIR FRAME CLEANING

The last part of preparation for the frame is to clean and revive the frame. For this I use a mixture of methylated spirit, white spirit and linseed oil, shaking equal parts of each ingredient together in a jar or bottle. You might want to wear gloves when you apply the solution to the chair frame. You can buy clean and revive solution ready mixed.

**Step 1** – Apply the clean and revive solution to the frame using 0000 wire wool, really rubbing the mixture into the wood. This will clean the wood and revive the original finish; it won't change the overall look of the chair or strip the original polish. Cover the whole chair, working into any dirty or scratched areas.

**Step 2** – Wipe any excess off with a cloth or flannel, making sure you rub in and remove any of the clean and revive solution. The illustration shows the difference between the revived wood and the original. The cane and chair are now ready to begin weaving. I've used some tape to show the cleaned and original wooden rails.

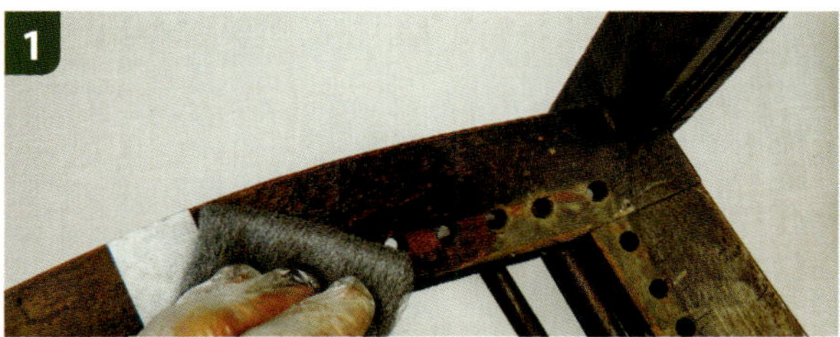
Applying the clean and revive mixture.

Cleaned and uncleaned frame.

CHAPTER 2

# STANDARD SIX-WAY PATTERN

The Standard Six-Way pattern is probably the most familiar pattern known for caned furniture. It has earned a place in our collective design DNA and is commonly seen on fabric, stationery and clothing. The pattern's origins are unknown, although it is thought to have originated in India or China. Cane chairs were introduced into Europe by Portuguese traders during the seventeenth century. Charles II was given a carved ebony chair with a caned seat, initiating the popularisation of the novel style, which was then copied on walnut and beechwood chair frames throughout the UK. The pattern has been used on furniture in Europe ever since.

## METHOD – FIRST SETTING

Once you have prepared your chair frame and dampened down the cane, check the number of holes in the frame and use the table (Chapter 1) to select your combination of cane sizes. You are now ready to begin weaving the first setting. When weaving this pattern, all vertical strands are called the settings, all horizontal strands are called the weavings. The settings and weavings will be woven using the thinner-size cane.

Choose a long piece of cane, checking to make sure it doesn't have any breaks or weak spots. You will need to use the cane shiny side up, so do familiarise yourself with the look of the smooth shiny side and the fibrous slightly duller underside.

**Step 1** – Count the holes on the back rail of your chair or frame and locate the centre hole. If there is an even number, locate the two central holes. Mark these with two pegs. If there is an odd number of holes, use one peg to mark the centre. Repeat for the front rail. This will be particularly important for trapezium- or round-shaped frames. I always start in the centre of the front and back rails as it is important to keep these initial settings square to the chair frame – even on shaped frames the settings and weavings should all sit parallel to one another and be evenly spaced.

**Step 2** – Take the back rail peg out – if you have two, choose the left- or right-hand one. Place the cane shiny side up in the hole, from the top with at least 12cm of cane through the hole and then place a peg in the hole to hold the cane in place.

**Step 3** – Hold the cane with the shiny side between your thumb and forefinger and feed the strand back through, so that you end up holding the very end of the cane with your thumb and forefinger. This should make sure that the cane is not twisted and remains shiny side up during the weaving process.

Completed cane chairs; Victorian dining chair and bentwood chair with a circular seat and back, and sample frame.

It is good to get used to doing this on the more straightforward parts of the weaving process as it will really help to stop the rattan from twisting as the weaving gets more complicated. You can then put the loose end of the cane into the parallel hole on the front rail of the chair. Pull it tight from the underneath and when it is drum tight, put a peg in the hole to hold the cane taut.

**Step 4** – Bring the end of the cane up from below to the top of the chair rail, through the next hole along to the right. As you pull the cane through, be careful not to get it twisted, especially as the loop between holes tightens. Pull the cane all the way and make sure the loop on the underside of the frame is not twisted. As you become more accomplished you will be able to feel this rather than having to look each time! Hold the cane taut and move the peg from the previous hole into the hole the cane has just been threaded through. This will be a 'working peg', meaning it will move as you weave the settings. It is important to peg the cane each time it comes through a hole. This keeps the tension and allows you to have both hands free for feeding the long length of cane back through your thumb and forefinger, then take it to the back of the frame and feed it into the corresponding hole. Pull it tight and then peg with the working peg. Continue with this until you reach the last hole – do not weave into the corner holes, these need to stay clear for the crossings (the diagonals).

**Step 5** – You can now repeat this process for the left-hand side of the frame. This is where the first setting finishes. If you have come to the end of the length of cane, before you complete the section

Centre pegged holes.

First cane held with a peg.

Centre cane pegged at both ends.

First setting in progress.

make sure you have a 'tail' of at least 12cm going through to the underneath of the chair. Then use the working peg to hold it tight. This working peg will now stay in this hole, and you can begin a new piece of cane, held with a new peg (*see* Step 3). This new cane will go into the hole next to the one you have just finished. Then continue weaving the settings until you reach one hole from the corner hole.

Completed first setting.

## METHOD – FIRST WEAVING

The 'weavings' refer to all the horizontal strands of cane. You will be using the same size cane as you did for the first setting. It is important to get the cane sizes right otherwise the pattern will look unbalanced and become crowded. All the strands of cane which make up the final woven panel should sit flat; using the correct size cane is crucial for achieving this. The first weaving will sit over the top of all the first settings and is threaded between the holes on the side rails of the chair frame. It is helpful that there isn't any actual weaving in and out at this stage as it will give you a chance to become familiar with how the cane feels to work with and how it may twist, before the weaving process becomes more complex.

**Step 1** – You can begin at the back of the chair seat on the left- or right-hand side rail. Start one hole down from the corner hole. These will usually be left clear for the crossings stage. I prefer to start at the back as it's easier and more comfortable to work towards oneself. Place your cane shiny side up into the first side hole, thread a 12cm tail into the hole. Peg the cane, then feed the strand of cane back through your thumb and forefinger. Thread the end into the corresponding hole on the opposite side of the frame and peg with a working peg. Make sure it is sitting flat and taut over the top of the first setting. Bring the end of the cane through the next hole down and pull it through, remembering to check that the cane loop isn't twisted underneath the frame. Peg the cane with your working peg, using the same method as for the first setting. Continue down the sides of the frame threading and pegging each hole. If you run out of cane, peg the end, and then start with a new piece as previously described. You will finish one hole up from the corner holes.

Completed first weaving.

## METHOD – SECOND SETTING

This stage of weaving the pattern follows exactly the same route as the first setting. Make sure you use the same size cane as you have done for the first setting and weaving.

**Step 1** – You can start threading the strands from the left- or right-hand side. Work the cane over the top of the first setting and first weaving. Keep the cane taut and flat, using a working peg as you go. In preparation for the next stage of weaving, it's helpful if you can place the cane to the right of the previous settings. To achieve this, as the cane comes out of the hole from below, place it to the right and peg it to hold it in position. Continue to pass the cane through your thumb and forefinger to keep it flat. If you need to go into a hole which already has a peg in it holding a tail, remove the peg while you weave the next cane and then replace the peg to hold the tail tight.

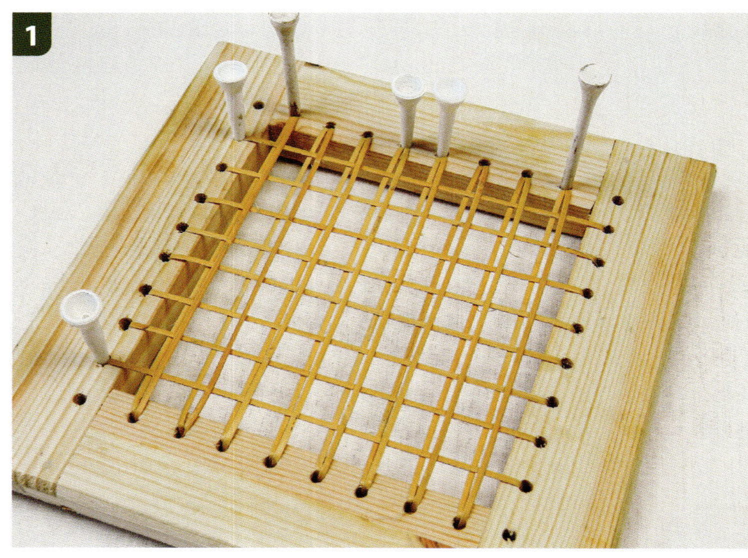

Completed second setting.

## METHOD – SECOND WEAVING

The second weaving follows the same layout as the first weaving, so all horizontals are caned from side to side. Use the same size cane as you did for the previous weaving. This stage is where we begin to actually weave the canes and it will start to bring all the previous stages together in a tight woven surface. You will get an idea of the layout of the final pattern and hopefully get a pleasing result as the grid comes together. I'd recommend using a short length of cane for this stage to begin with, as it's important to understand how this stage is woven. If you use a long piece of cane, you'll spend a lot of time trying to untwist it. You can move on to using longer lengths as you become more familiar with this stage of the process.

**Step 1** – I usually begin this stage in the centre of the side rails. It can get tight at the top and bottom edges, so I always find it useful to begin in the middle so that the cane settings I'm weaving under and over have 'opened up' by the time I reach the edges. You will need to weave the second weaving from left to right and vice versa, but I'm going to explain how to begin working the cane from right to left. Check the piece of cane you are going to use for this stage before starting – if you pass it through your fingers, you may feel small shards of fibrous cane running in one direction; use the cane in the direction that these run smooth. You will need the cane to be flexible for this stage. Thread a short length into a hole in the centre (or thereabouts) of the right-hand side rail. Leave a tail and put a peg in to secure it. Place one hand under the chair seat and hold on to the cane with the other hand on the top of the woven panel. You may find a straight bodkin helpful to open the space between the two settings.

**Step 2** – This horizontal row will sit below the first weaving. Take the end of the cane you are holding over the second setting, then down under the first setting next to it (use the hand below the seat to bring it down) and then pass it back up so you're in position to repeat this. Pull the cane tight and you will see it forms a nice intersection of the two settings and two weavings. Repeat until you reach the end of the row. Begin by weaving these

Starting the second weaving.

Using a shell bodkin for the second weaving.

intersections one at a time; once you have got the pattern you can weave two or three and then pull the cane tight. It is essential to practise feeding the cane back through the thumb and forefinger to keep it flat, the shiny side up and untwisted. As well as threading the cane from the underneath to the surface with your hands, you may find the shell bodkin useful for guiding the cane in and out of the settings. Use the channel in the shell bodkin to guide the cane and pull it through with your thumb.

**Step 3** – When you reach the end of the first row, place the end into the hole and come up the next hole down. You will then be weaving the same sequence but the other way, so the end of the cane will go under the first setting then up and over the second setting. It is important that these rows are pulled tight enough – if not, the second setting will look bumpy and it won't sit flat next to the other stages of weaving. Weave all the rows until you reach the front rail and then repeat to weave all the rows up to the back rail. When this stage is complete, you may want to straighten out some of the rows. You can use the bodkin for this. You will find that the crossings will pull everything into position, but you get a clearer picture of the pattern with a little bit of straightening out. Remember this is an open weave so don't push the pairs of settings and weavings together. There should be a gap between them.

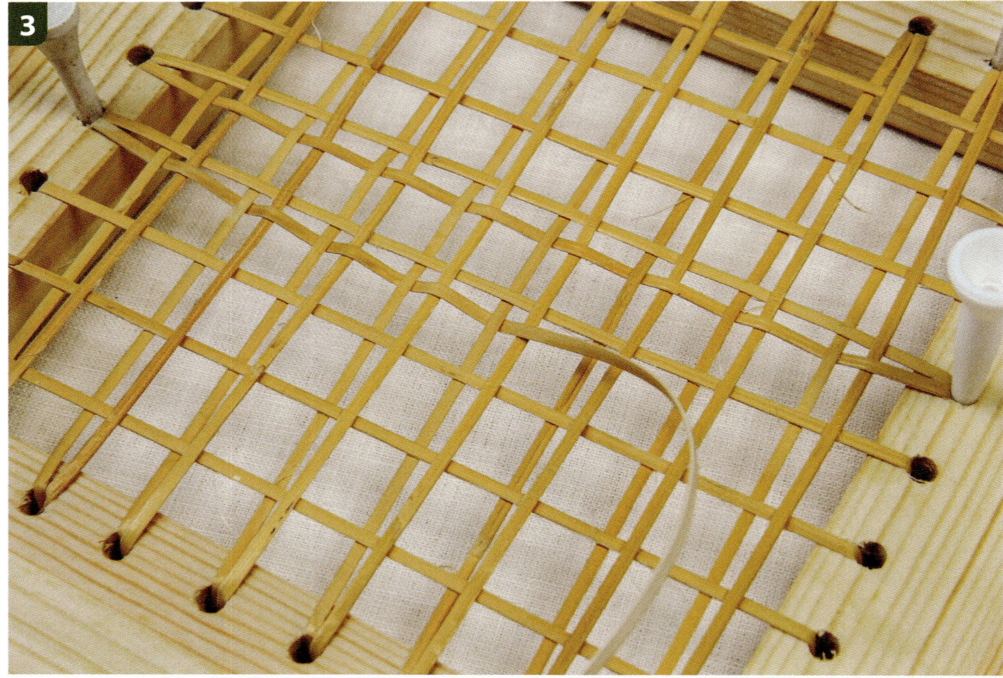


The second weaving.

## METHOD – FIRST CROSSING

This is the first of two diagonal strands you will weave. You will need to use the thicker size of cane for these final stages. From now on you'll treat the settings and weavings as pairs. You either go under or over the pair; if you're coming up in between them, the pattern won't be correct. Also make sure you are going under and over the settings and weavings in the correct order – if not the crossings won't sit flat but will twist in the corner intersections, causing the seat to be bumpy rather than all stages sitting flat and smooth. The directions for the crossings are sometimes referred to by geographical directions, 'London to Liverpool' or 'Yeovil to York'!

**Step 1** – I like to begin at the corner hole at the back left-hand corner of the chair. You will be weaving forward towards the front right-hand corner. As before, you can use a short piece of cane until you get used to the pattern you are weaving. Put the cane in the hole leaving a tail underneath of 12cm. Take the end of the cane – I like to bend a slight curve in the end. You may also like to try using the shell bodkin for this stage. Personally, I find that the curved end of the cane works well but try both ways and see which suits you best. Using the curved end of the cane, weave it under the first pair of settings sitting to the right of the corner hole.

**Step 2** – Pull the cane under and then allow the cane to sit over the pair of weavings, moving in the direction of the front of the chair seat. Then weave the curved end of the cane under the next pair of settings in the direction of the right-hand side of the chair. Pull the cane tight and you will see it is beginning to straighten the pairs of settings and weavings. If you want to use the shell bodkin, place the curved end of the bodkin under the pair of settings; you can use the channel in the tool to feed the cane under the pair, then use your thumb to pull it through. Continue along the whole diagonal row. It is important to finish in the correct hole – unless your chair has a square seat it's unlikely the crossing will finish in the front right-hand corner hole, so follow the weaving process as described until you reach the last setting or weaving and make sure you take the crossing over or under. One of the most common errors in caning chair seats is how the edges are finished. You must weave the pattern to the end. If you miss going over or under the very last setting or weaving, the crossing canes will bend back in an awkward way. Once the second crossing is in, this will make a 'Y' or 'V' shape at the edge. This would need to be corrected. If the pattern is woven correctly, you will see a pleasing 'X' shape at the edges of the caned panel. This can be confusing,

Starting the first crossing.

The first completed crossing line.

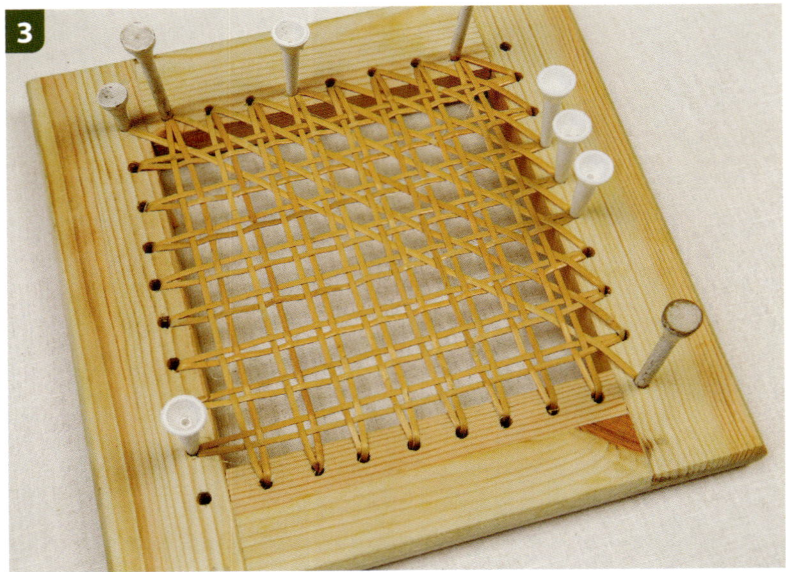
Half of the first crossing woven.

Completed first crossing.

particularly on trapezium-shaped seats, but with experience you'll begin to spot this edge detail.

**Step 3** – Once you reach the end of the row, put the cane in the appropriate hole. If you are on the front rail bring it up to the right, or if you are on the corner or side rail bring the end up the next hole along, towards the back right-hand corner. Repeat the process as before, over the weaving pairs, under the setting pairs, making sure your edges are finished correctly. Complete the rows working towards the back right-hand corner.

**Step 4** – It is usual to have two crossings in the corner holes. Where the two canes go into one hole it is referred to as a 'fisheye'. To complete the first crossing, begin in the top left-hand corner hole and weave the rows as before towards the front right-hand corner. You will need a single cross between the last two holes in the corners.

## METHOD – SECOND CROSSING

This is the last stage of the Standard Six-Way pattern; by now the woven surface will be feeling strong and secure. The second crossing will weave under and over the opposite settings and weavings to the first crossing. The result is that each setting and weaving pair is enclosed by the crossings, which really adds to the overall strength and balanced look of the pattern. You may find that the frame holes are getting tight now, so I'd recommend using the bodkin to open some space in the holes. Make sure your edges are all finished correctly to achieve a cross. If the pattern isn't fully woven or is incorrectly woven at the edges, this will really affect the overall strength of the seat.

**Step 1** – Use the thicker-size cane as you did for the first crossing, again treating the settings and weavings pairs as one, so no threading in between the pairs. Begin at the front left-hand corner and you will be weaving back towards the back right-hand corner. Place a cane tail into the hole and secure it with a peg. Bend a curve into the other end of the cane and begin by going over the first crossing, and then under the first pair of horizontals. You will find you are also going under the first crossing. Pull the cane through and then moving up, go over the first setting pair – this will also take you over the first crossing.

**Step 2** – Continue along the diagonal line towards the back right-hand corner, check that you are going under each weaving pair and over each setting pair. As you finish each row of diagonals it is important to make sure your edges are finishing correctly. The edges should finish with an 'X'; if the edge shape is forming a 'V' then the weaving hasn't been completed. This may also show up as the cane at the end of the row bending backwards. A tip for this would be to weave the pattern wherever there is an option to, don't finish in a frame hole if there's still an opportunity to go over or under a pair of weavings or settings.

Starting the second crossing.

The completed second crossing.

## Trapezium Frames

The previous instructions are for working on a square or rectangle frame. Much of the furniture you may find which is suitable for caning was designed and made in the Victorian and Edwardian eras. There is a common style of small bedroom chair which was made in large numbers in the furniture workshops based in High Wycombe during this period, usually trapezium-shaped and very often with additional bowed fronts.

The trapezium shape will either have the same number of holes along the front and back rails or there will be more holes along the wider front rail. The weaving process is the same for these shaped frames as already described, however there are some additional instructions needed for settings and weavings.

**Step 1** – Begin by counting the number of holes along the back and front rails of the frame. If the frame has the same number of holes along the front and back, you can weave the pattern as previously described. The holes are a bit closer together on the back rail so the pattern will be tighter. If you have more holes on the front rail than the back, count the number and find the centre hole on both the front and back rails. Mark each centre hole with a peg. As described before, if you have an even number of holes mark the two centre holes. Starting in the centre of the back rail, weave the first setting as described previously (first setting). As you work out from the centre, you'll begin to see that soon you will run out of holes along the back rail but still have holes on the front. You will need to add short strands which will run from the front rail holes and finish on the side rails. These short strands must run parallel to the settings already in place and should be the same distance apart. Make sure the short strands are an equal distance from the previous settings all the way to the finishing holes on the side rail. Place as many short strands as you need to fill the holes on the front rail on the first side. Leave the corner holes free.

**Step 2** – Complete the first setting on the other side of the panel, again leaving the corner holes free. You may find that the 'fill-in' strands don't finish in the same holes on each side rail. This reflects the anomalies in the spacing between the drilled holes. This job would have been done by hand so the space between holes is not always even. It is more important for the

Half of the first setting for a trapezium frame.

The completed first setting for a trapezium frame.

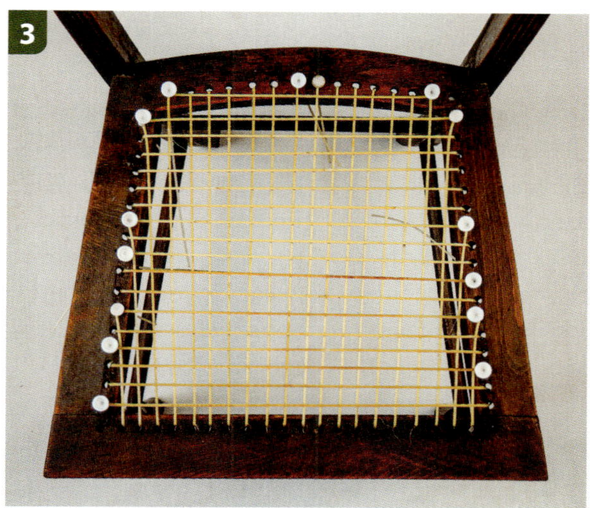

The completed first weaving for a trapezium frame.

Finished Six-Way caned pattern on a trapezium chair.

Frame edges with doubles and crosses.

setting strands to run parallel and be evenly spaced, than for the extra canes to finish in matching holes, and best not to create big loops on the underside of the caned seat, so only loop between two holes which are next to each other.

**Step 3** – The first weaving goes on as described previously. If you have a curved front or back rail, you will also need to add some fill-in strands at the front and back where needed.

**Steps 4 and 5** – Weave all the other stages as before. Remember to use the thicker cane for the crossings if you are using two sizes. Take every opportunity to weave the ends of the crossing strands into the settings and weavings. This is so that you achieve 'crosses' along the edges of the caned panel. You will see that on the sloped side rails I have missed some holes and doubled up the crossings on other holes to achieve a tidy edge. Some areas do achieve the crosses on the sloped rails. Where one end of the crossings doubles up, they will be single at the other ends.

## ROUND FRAMES

It is quite common to come across chairs with round seats or backs. The Thonet bentwood chair company began producing caned furniture in the 1850s and the familiar café-style caned chairs are still produced today. Many of their classic designs including the café chair have round seats. I was shown a different order of weaving stages by my dad, who taught me chair caning – I find that using this process for caning a circular seat helps to keep the lines straight. It is of course absolutely fine to use the traditional process if you prefer!

**Step 1** – Find the centre back and front holes as explained before. On a round seat, I would recommend measuring between the chair back upright posts to find the centre hole. Then count a matching number of holes around each side of the frame to find the centre front rail hole. Weave the first setting with short fill-in strands added onto the sides as described in the section on trapezium frames. You will need to miss caning into some holes, to keep the settings parallel and as evenly spaced as the holes allow.

**Step 2** – Count the holes from the front and back centres to work out where the left- and right-hand side centre holes are. Begin your first weaving starting from these side centre holes. Work towards the back adding in short fill-in strands and then work to the front, adding in the fill-in strands to complete the first weaving.

**Step 3** – If you are using two sizes of cane, use the thicker size now, because you are going to put your first crossing in. Start in the back left-hand corner, weave under the first setting and over the first weaving. Check your edges, make sure that you weave the crossings through the settings and weavings wherever possible. You will also see you have some holes with double ends and some holes with no ends.

**Step 4** – Proceed with the second setting positioned as previously described. You will be laying the cane over the first setting, first weaving and first crossing.

**Step 5** – Proceed with the second weaving as previously described; this weaving will be going under the first crossing and setting, and over the second setting. Lastly, weave in the second crossing. The cane will go under the pairs of weavings and over the pairs of settings. Check all your edges – it is likely you will have more doubles (fisheyes) going into the rail holes as you have worked around the round frame and more missed holes. Let the cane follow the settings and weavings to the appropriate hole. The result will be a few edge crosses front, back and sides, with doubles and misses in between.

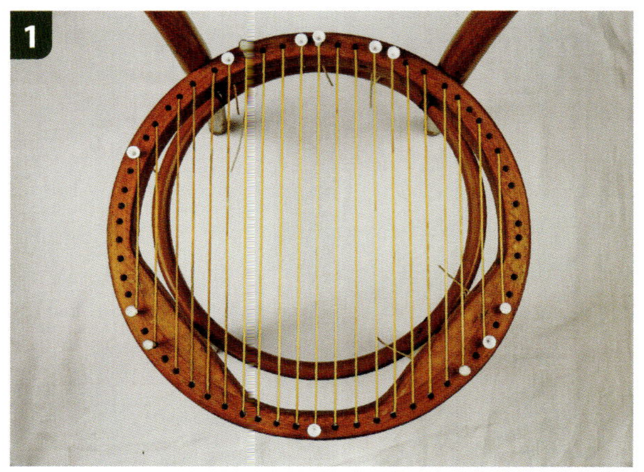


The first setting for a round frame.

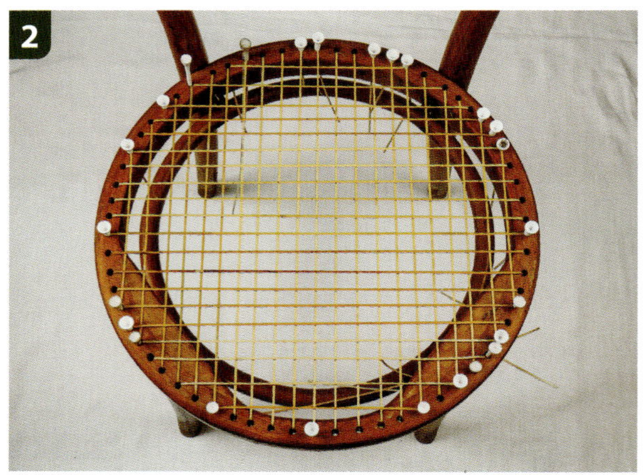


The first weaving on a round frame.

The first crossing on a round frame.

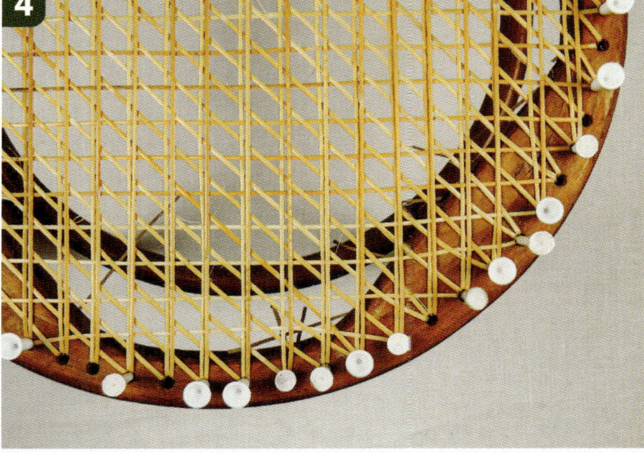


The second setting on a round frame.

5

Completed round chair seat.

CHAPTER 3

# PEGGING AND BEADING

There are various ways to finish your newly caned seat, each technique involving pegging or beading the open holes on the chair frame. You'll have noticed how tight the completed woven seat is – however, this still needs a final fix!

Up until the 1850s or thereabouts, cane seats were simply finished with a peg in each hole and the tails of cane under the frame were trimmed. After this date a more decorative beading finish was seen more often. There are a few different iterations of this finish – I would recommend studying which style was originally used on your chair and copy that. If you received the chair without any cane, it may be worth trying to date the frame and then using the appropriate method.

Some chair caners prefer to trim the tails from the bottom of the seat after they have completed the pegging, others prefer to trim them before pegging. I trim the tail ends before I peg as a little pull and snip allows the cut end to spring back inside the hole. You won't feel sharp cut ends (known traditionally as 'dragon's teeth') when you run your fingers over the holes. Cutting after the holes have been pegged means the cut end is fixed; if it protrudes, you will feel the sharp end of the cane.

Once the seat is complete with pegs or beading, you may notice that there are fine hairs from the fibrous canes you have woven the panel with. If they are large, you can snip them off. Some brave souls deal with these by taking a lighter flame and running it over the underneath of the seat, causing the fine hairs to frizzle as they burn off. If you choose this method, please don't hold the flame too close to the seat as it will very easily burn! In my experience these fine hairs tend to wear away once the chair starts to be used, so I just leave them.

Various techniques for beading and pegging.

## METHOD – PEGGING (CENTRE CANE)

Pegs were probably originally made from wood which was split and whittled to the appropriate size. It is more common nowadays for these fixing pegs to be made from the 'centre cane'. I've outlined both methods using centre cane and wooden pegs.

**Step 1** – Remove all the tees or working pegs. Turn the chair upside down and place it flat on a table or work bench top. Using your side cutters, preferably ones with a pointed end, pull one of the long tails down firmly through the hole. Keep hold of it and snip the tail off with the point of the side cutters, as far inside the hole as possible. The cut end should be just inside the hole and should not be felt protruding. Continue for all tail ends.

**Step 2** – Turn the chair back upright. The fixing pegs will be inserted into the frame holes from the top side of the seat. Select an appropriate size of centre cane – if it's too thick you won't be able to press the end into the frame hole, if it's too thin it will push through the hole. The pegs should not fill the full depth of the hole but should sit about halfway down. Take a cut piece of centre cane (30–40cm) and press the end firmly into the first hole. When it is in as far as you can press, cut the top of it flat with the side cutters.

**Step 3** – Use your hole-clearing tool, or a blunt 6in (15cm) nail to tap the pegs in fully so that they sit flush to the top of the hole. If you use the hole-clearing tool, tap it with a wooden mallet; if you use a nail, tap it with a metal hammer. The tops of the pegs should be flat and flush with the frame.

Trimming the cane tails.

Centre cane pegs.

Pegs flattened with a hole clearer.

## METHOD – PEGGING (WOODEN PEGS)

**Step 1** – Remove all the golf tees or holding pegs. To make these wooden pegs, you will need a small block of soft wood such as pine, approximately 15cm × 5cm × 5cm. Stand the block upright on a work bench and use a knife and a hammer to split the block. Keep splitting until you have long pegs, just a little larger than the hole in the chair.

**Step 2** – If you need to whittle the square ends off to get them to fit into the holes, use the knife to do this. Always swipe away from your body with the knife. Once you have made the long pegs follow Step 3 and 4 from the 'Pegging (centre cane)' section.

Splitting wood to make pegs.

Pegging the frame holes with wooden pegs.

## METHOD – PEGGING FOR THE BACK OR ARMS

Once you have woven a cane panel for the back or arms of a chair, you will have noticed that the weaving loops are on display on the back. It is crucial that these are tight, that they only go from one hole to the next and that they are not twisted. You also need to have one loop between each hole. If you don't have a loop between each hole, follow the steps below.

**Step 1** – Remove all the golf tees or working pegs. Before you snip all the tails, check the back of the chair to see if you have any loops between the holes missing. If you do have a missing loop, take a long tail from the back of the panel, next to the missing loop and thread it to the face side of the seat, through the hole which will create a loop between holes.

**Step 2** – On the face side of the caned panel, hold this tail tightly while you insert the peg. Snip the peg – it is important not to let the loop underneath loosen as you press the peg into the frame hole. Snip the tail so it is flush with the peg.

Making a loop with a tail of cane.

Pegging and trimming the tail on the front of the chair.

## METHOD – BEADING (EVERY HOLE)

You will need to use two different sizes of cane to finish the chairs using beading; 3.9–4mm cane is used for the edging and 2.00–2.1mm for the 'couching' (the stitched loops which hold the beading cane in place). You can bead every hole or use a combination of couching and pegs. I've outlined both methods below. If your cane panel is round, it is best to use just one piece of beading cane and finish with one peg at the centre back of the panel. If the panel is square or trapezium, finish with four pegs in the four corners.

**Step 1** – For square, rectangle or trapezium frames, cut four pieces of 4mm cane the length of each edge of the seat plus 10cm or so. Select two or three long lengths of 2.1mm cane. Make sure the cane is soaked and kept damp and pliable by wrapping it in a cloth or towel (*see* Chapter 1). Remove all golf tees or working pegs and trim the tail ends as described at the start of this chapter. Place a golf tee or peg in each of the four corners. Starting at the back left-hand hole, remove the peg and put the end of the 3.9–4mm cane into the corner hole, leave a 5cm tail and then put the peg back in the hole to hold the cane in position.

**Step 2** – Take the long piece of 2.1mm cane and thread 15cm into the first hole along from the corner, feed the length back through your thumb and forefinger and then thread the other end into the same hole. Thread the end over the top of the 4mm cane so that as you pull it through, it forms a loop over the top of the beading cane. Pull the loop in tight so that the beading cane sits flat to the frame. Take the long end of the 2.1mm cane and thread it up through the next hole along, pull it all the way through and make sure that the loop on the underside of the seat is tight to the frame. Take the end of the cane over the beading cane and back down through the same hole, pull the loop in tight. You can use a bodkin to help get the loop tight over the beading cane.

**Step 3** – Repeat this for all the holes until you reach the last one before the back right-hand side corner hole. When you reach this point, thread the next piece of 3.9–4mm cane into the corner hole and put the tee back in to hold it. Then make the last

Starting the beading.

Looping in the beading.

loop with the thin cane and cut it to leave a 15cm tail. Continue looping over the 4mm cane, working towards the next corner hole.

**Step 4** – Complete this method for all four sides. To finish, you will need to trim the tails of the 4mm cane and put a fixing peg into each corner hole.

**Step 5** – Lastly, tie a simple knot to fix in the thinner cane on the underside of the frame. Take the tail end and thread it under the loop next to it, repeat this, and to finish, bring the end through the loop to make a small knot. Cut the end as close as you can to the frame.

Beading on the corner.

Completed beading.

The knot to tie off the beading.

## METHOD – PEGGING AND BEADING (ALTERNATE HOLES)

The method for this finish is the same as described in the previous instructions, however before couching in the beading cane you will need to peg every other hole. This finish gives the added benefit of having half of the holes pegged, which gives strength to the woven seat and a pleasing look. Begin with a golf tee or peg in the four corner holes and work out a balanced look for the alternate pegs and couched stitches. If you have an odd number of holes between the corners you will end up with a couched stitch at each end of the row, which will look symmetrical. If you have an even number of holes between corners, you will need to have two couched holes next to each other. This pair can either sit next to the corner, or you can centralise them to give a balanced look. Whichever you choose, it is best if all four rails are matching.

**Step 1** – Follow Steps 1–3 from 'Pegging (centre cane)' or Steps 1 and 2 from 'Pegging (wooden pegs)'. For this method you will only peg every other hole.

**Step 2** – Follow Steps 1–5 from 'Beading (every hole)', only couching every other hole with the thinner cane, which hasn't been filled with a peg.

Every other rail hole pegged.

Completed alternate hole beading.

## METHOD – PEGGING AND BEADING (WITHOUT COUCHING)

For this method the beading cane is folded and pegged into each hole, but you can also use this method of beading every other hole. If you are doing every other hole, peg every other hole to begin as described in 'Pegging and Beading (alternate holes)'. Make sure the cane is damp and pliable before you begin.

**Step 1** – Follow Steps 1 and 2 from 'Pegging'. For square, rectangle or trapezium frames, cut four pieces of beading cane the length of each edge of the seat plus 10cm or so. For round seats cut a piece which will go all the way around the frame. Make sure the cane is soaked and kept damp and pliable by wrapping it in a cloth or towel (*see* Chapter 1). Select a suitable size of centre cane for the holes. If your seat is square, rectangle or trapezium, put four tees or working pegs into the four corners; if it is round, put one tee in the centre back hole. Insert one end of the 3.9–4mm cane into one hole marked with a tee, leave a tail of 5cm. Carefully curve the 4mm cane and insert it into the next hole along.

**Step 2** – Push the centre cane into the hole over this loop as far as it will go. Snip it with the side cutters and tap down with the hole clearer or blunt nail.

**Step 3** – Repeat this method until each hole has beading cane and a peg in it.

Starting the pegging and beading variation.

Pegging the beading cane.

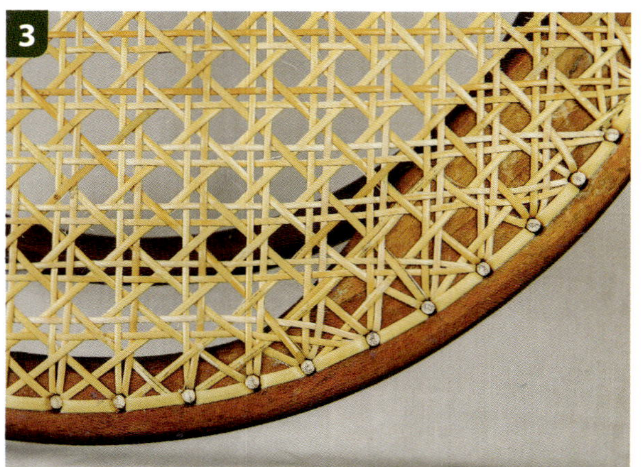

The completed pegging and beading variation.

## METHOD – PEGGING BLIND HOLES

Blind holes describe a type of cane furniture where the holes in the frame are not drilled all the way through to the other side. This type of caning is usually reserved for the arms or back of chairs as it does not have the strength of a standard cane panel that is woven and looped through full frame holes. I will be outlining the method for caning a chair which has 'blind' holes in the next chapter. Blind holes can be simply pegged using the same method as described in 'Pegging (centre cane)' or 'Pegging (wooden pegs)'.

## METHOD – BEADING BLIND HOLES

You can use this method to bead every hole or every other hole if you want to use the one peg, one couched hole method. If you are pegging every other hole, get the alternate pegs into the frame holes first. This is the only occasion that glue is used to secure a cane panel. It is quite fiddly so make sure you have plenty of time!

**Step 1** – Cut four pieces of beading cane the length of each edge of the cane panel plus 10cm or so if your panel is square or rectangle; if it is circular, one long piece will be needed. Select two or three long lengths of 2.1mm cane. Make sure the cane is soaked and kept damp and pliable by wrapping it in a cloth or towel (*see* Chapter 1). As the holes do not go all the way through to the back of the frame to allow for a loop, each beading stitch will need to be glued into place. Remove all tees or working pegs and use a bodkin to make sure the holes have space. Place a golf tee or peg in each of the four corners. If square, start at the back left-hand hole, remove the peg and put the end of the beading cane into the hole and then put the peg back in to hold the cane in position. If circular, do the same but in the centre bottom hole (this is a chair back). Check the hole depth with your bodkin and using 2.1mm cane, cut some small lengths just under double the depth of the hole. Gently curve these into a 'U' or hairpin shape. Prepare ten or so. Half-fill five or so holes from the left-hand corner with wood glue.

**Step 2** – Lay the 3.9–4mm cane flat over the holes and then take one of the 2.1mm 'U'-shaped canes, put one end down into the glued hole, bring the other end over the beading cane and press this down into the hole on the other side. Do this for the five holes filled with glue, then fill the next five holes with glue.

**Step 3** – Repeat this until all the holes have been beaded with the 'U'-shaped canes. You may need to adjust the length of the cane hairpins depending on the space available in each hole. The loops should be pressed in tightly and sit as flush to the frame as possible.

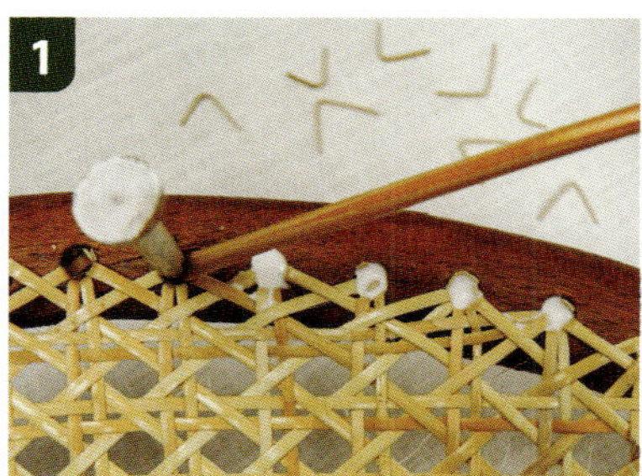

Hairpin canes for blind beading.

Hairpin canes holding beading cane in place.

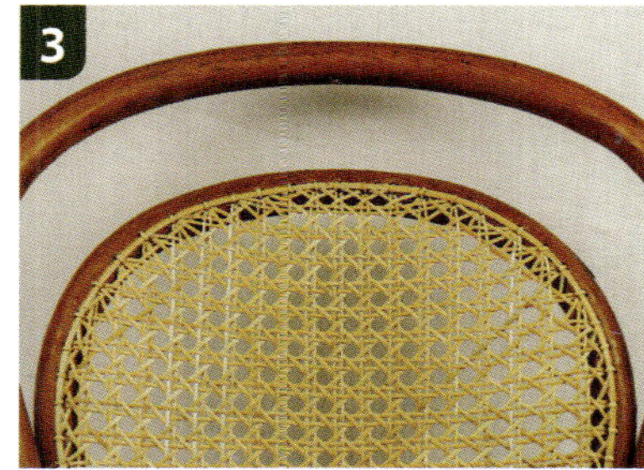

Complete beading for blind holes.

CHAPTER 4

# CURVED FRAMES, BLIND AND DOUBLE CANING

The Standard Six-Way pattern I have described so far relates particularly to dining or bedroom type chairs, which have flat panels. In this chapter I'm going to describe methods for replacing cane panels on some other types of chair shapes. The more you look at caned furniture, you will discover a wide variety of shapes and styles. Each shape comes with its own challenges and in this chapter, I'll outline some methods for dealing with these.

Many tub chairs were produced in the early 1800s. These have caned seats, backs and arms caned as curved single panels. Very often the caned seat was given added comfort with a squab cushion. The curved backs and seats seem to have been produced not only as the soft lines are aesthetically pleasing, but the curved lines are designed with an ergonomic purpose – to follow the contours of our bodies – making the chairs very comfortable to sit on.

Curved frames include tub chairs (seats or backs which have a curve horizontally and vertically) and double-curved seats known as 'Saddle' or 'S' shapes. There are a few ways to approach these shapes which I will outline. I've also recommended which type of chair I have found each method to work best on. Of course, you may try them and find you have your own preference. It is important to assess the tension of the cane as you weave; if pulled too tight the new panel won't follow the curved frame, it will stand proud and look as if it has popped up, making a convex dome shape. Once the tight panel begins to be used it will be likely to break as the canes are put under too much pressure, rather than the frame taking the pressure. There are also some instructions for using a weaving strap and a steamer, tools we haven't looked at yet.

Double caning is only used on seats and backs, very commonly seen on the Bergère type three-piece suites as well as a lot of French furniture, including head and foot boards.

All these types of furniture are generally woven in the Standard Six-Way pattern which you are already familiar with. There will be some variations in the order of weaving and other techniques to use when weaving curved frames, furniture with blind holes or items which are double caned.

All these styles are finished off using one of the pegging and beading techniques described in the previous chapter.

Cane chairs with curved frames; steamer chair, tub chair and Josef Hoffman Thonet 811 chair.

## METHOD – CURVED FRAME (TUB CHAIR)

These chairs are challenging. Not only will you be caning a large panel which makes up the back and both arms in one, but you will also need to navigate keeping the tension on this sizeable curved panel. You may need to tighten or loosen strands along the way, check at the end of each stage and adjust where necessary. Keep an eye on the back of the chairs to make sure loops are not twisted and are shiny side up. You want to finish with a loop between each hole where they are on display. These chairs as mentioned may also have a caned seat, so the bottom edge holes will be used for the seat too, therefore double the amount of cane ends will be going into these holes. I always cane the back and arm panels first as I find it easier to access this area without a caned seat panel in the way. I also like to complete the harder part of the chair first, breezing through the relatively straightforward seat after the more challenging panel is complete!

**Step 1** – Before you strip the old cane away, do remember to take lots of photos and notes on the original placing of the cane. Look at the panel in profile so you can see how the existing cane follows the shape of the frame. On all shaped chairs it is important that the new cane follows the frame shape. Also make a note of the cane sizes used. This type of chair will most probably just be pegged to finish; this is because beading doesn't sit so well on the curved shapes and most of these chairs were made before it became popular. I am using all 2.4mm cane as this tub chair has just seven holes per 15cm. Locate and mark with a tee the centre holes on the top back and bottom seat rails. Working from these centre holes weave the first setting, using the methods outlined in Chapter 2. Follow the holes all the way around to the last holes in the arms on each side. If the arms are shaped, you may need to fill in as described in Chapter 2. This setting will follow the shape of the frame and ideally will be the shape for the finished cane panel. Make sure this stage is very tight and that the loops on the back of the frame are not twisted as they will be on display.

**Step 2** – Cane your first weaving; this should be placed behind the first setting. Be very careful not to pull it too tight as this will affect the curve shape. You can begin the first weaving at the bottom of the panel, next to the seat. Add in any short strands you need to as you get to the top. Keep the weavings horizontal.

Tub chair, first setting.

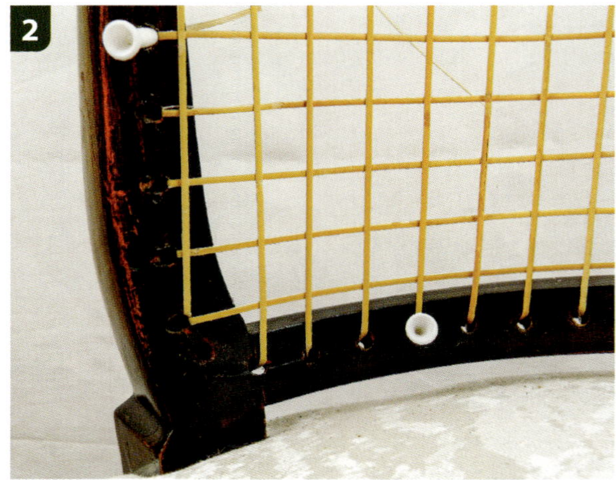


First weaving.

**Step 3** – Weave the second setting behind both the first setting and the first weaving, pull this stage tight and sit the cane to the right of the first setting.

**Step 4** – Cane the second weaving, below the first weaving. It will go over the first setting and under the second setting, the same process as in Chapter 2. Begin at the bottom of the panel and work up, keeping the lines straight. Don't pull them too tight as you don't want to pull the curved shape out of line with the chair frame.

**Step 5** – Weave in the two crossings as described for the standard pattern in Chapter 2. Then tidy the ends and loops and peg each hole.

Second setting.

Second weaving.

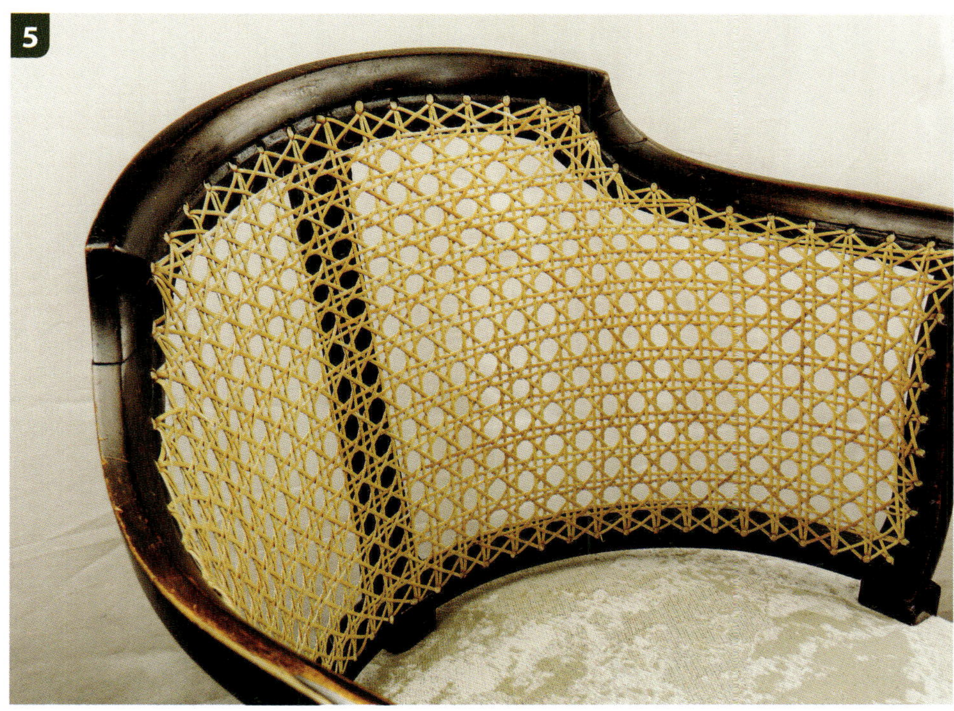


Complete tub chair with two crossings.

## METHOD – CURVED FRAME (TUB CHAIR) ALTERNATIVE METHOD 1

**Step 1** – Place both settings in at the same time. Make sure they are tight.

**Step 2** – Cane your first weaving; this should be placed behind the setting on the left and over the setting on the right. Then weave in the second weaving. Continue working up from the bottom of the panel. Be very careful not to pull the weavings too tight as this will affect the curve shape. Add in any short strands you need to as you get to the top. Keep the weavings horizontal. To finish, add in the crossings as usual.

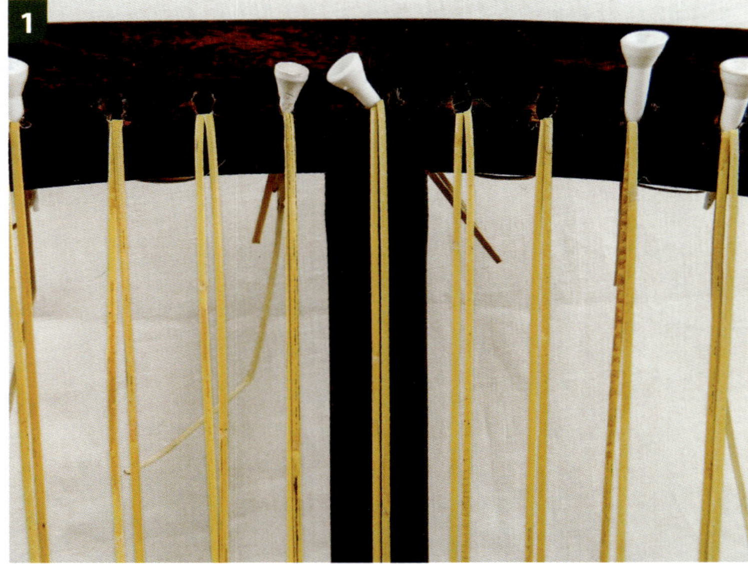

Tub chair with double settings.

Tub chair with double weavings.

## METHOD – CURVED FRAME (TUB CHAIR) ALTERNATIVE METHOD 2

The different order of weaving listed below really helps to keep the tension and keep everything in place, especially if you are working on a large back and arm panel.

**Step 1** – Place the first setting and first weaving as described previously in Curved Frame Step 1 and 2, above. Weave the first crossing from the bottom right-hand corner, where the arm and seat rails and uprights meet, cane up to the top left-hand corner (London to Liverpool). This crossing will run under the first weaving and over the first setting. Placing the crossing at this point will stabilise the first setting and weaving. Don't pull these too tight but allow the strands to follow the shape created by the first setting.

**Step 2** – The second setting will run behind all the previous three stages. Pull these tight to maintain the curve shape and place them to the right of the first setting. They should also finish in the same holes as the first setting.

**Step 3** – The second weaving should be placed below the first weaving. Then sit over the crossing, over the first setting, and finally under the second setting. The final crossing will weave in, as described in Chapter 2. Tidy the ends and loops on the back of the chair and peg off.

Tub chair with one setting, weaving and crossing.

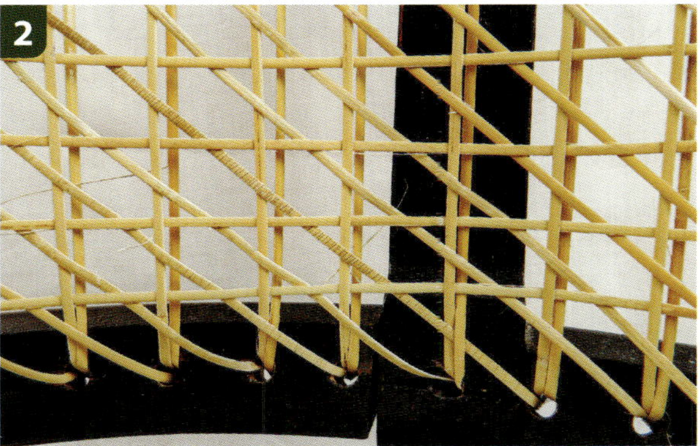

Tub chair second setting.

Complete tub chair with second weaving and crossing.

## METHOD – CURVED FRAME (SADDLE OR 'S' SHAPE)

This type of seat or back is commonly seen on various types of folding cane furniture but also on some non-folding Victorian chairs. They typically have a concave dip in the middle of the frame which straightens out at the front and back, sometimes called an 'S' shape. This dip means there is a double-curved shape to weave. It is very helpful to photograph this type of panel side-on so you are aware what the final shape of the caned panel should be. You can use any of the three methods described for the tub chair, however this method works very well for these smaller panels.

**Step 1** – Your first setting will be woven horizontally to describe the curves in the frame. Also weave the second setting now and place it forward from the first setting. Use the thinner cane size as usual.

**Step 2** – The next stage is to add both weavings at the same time. You can weave the first weaving under the first setting, over the second, and then your second weaving does the opposite, over the first setting then under the second setting. Continue weaving alternate weavings, allowing them to sit loosely enough so that the S-shape curves defined by the settings aren't lost by over-pulling the canes. See the next section on using the steamer tool or strap to speed up this process.

**Step 3** – Use the thicker-size cane if using for the crossings. It can help with the curved shape to weave each of the pairs of crossing directions at the same time. Weave one London to Liverpool then one Yeovil to York until all the crossings are complete. Finish off the ends and peg as described in Chapter 2.

'S'-shape frame, first and second horizontal setting.

'S'-shape frame, two weavings.

'S'-shape frame, two crossings.

## METHOD – CURVED FRAME (SADDLE AND 'S' SHAPE) ALTERNATIVE METHOD USING A STEAMER OR THREADER TOOL

The threader tool, alternatively called a steamer, is usually made from thin, flexible metal. They sometimes have a wooden handle and a threading hole in the metal end, or if there is no handle there will be a hole in each end. I'll explain how to use this tool below. A second tool which is used in a similar way is a flat strap which I make from a length of the flat packing tape you get on parcels, or the flat cardboard tape upholsterers use. You will need one piece which is cut twice the length of the panel you are caning. Make a hole in the centre of the strap. These tools can be used on normal flat seats or backs, but are particularly useful on these 'S'-shape frames where you have long weavings to cane simultaneously.

### Steamer Tool

**Step 1** – Place the two settings in at the same time, described in Step 1 in the 'Method – Curved Frame (saddle or 'S' shape)' section. You will need two long pieces of cane, one pegged in on the right-hand side hole and the other pegged in the opposite hole on the left-hand side. Begin on the left-hand side and weave the steamer under the first setting and over the second setting all the way over to the right-hand side. Thread the left-hand side cane into the steamer hole and bend the end 1–2cm so it holds in place. Pull the steamer through to the right. Take the end of the cane out of the steamer hole and then put it into the frame hole on the right-hand side with the other weaving cane and a peg. Loop it under and peg it in the next hole along the frame.

**Step 2** – Move the steamer up towards the back of the panel and weave it over the first setting and under the second, the opposite to the cane you just placed in using the steamer. Use the long cane which was originally pegged on the right-hand side, and thread the end into the steamer before you pull it across to the left-hand side. Peg the cane into the left-hand hole. Bring the long cane end back up to the top of the frame through the next hole up (on the left-hand side) and weave it in place using the steamer as described. Continue this sequence until all the weavings are in place. Don't pull these weavings too tight but allow them to keep the curved shape created by the settings.

First weaving using a steamer tool.

Second weaving using a steamer tool.

## STRAP TOOL

**Step 1** – Begin with two long pieces of cane, one pegged in the left-hand side and one on the right-hand side. Begin on the left-hand side and weave the strap under the first setting and over the next, all the way across. The strap centre hole will now be next to the peg on the left-hand side. Thread the cane into the hole and pull the strap across to the right, only until the strap hole is next to the right-hand side peg. You will still have half the strap in between the weavings. Thread the end of the cane into the pegged hole and up through the next hole up.

**Step 2** – Move the strap up the panel to make space so that you can either hand cane or use the metal steamer tool to take the long cane from the right over to the left, under the setting and over the next. Put the cane into the frame hole and bring it up through the next hole up.

**Step 3** – Go back to the right-hand side and thread the long cane into the strap hole and pull it across to the left, stopping when the strap hole reaches the frame. Now you can continue the sequence from Step 1. The strap will remain woven into the caned panel until you finish. Once the weavings are completed, finish the crossings as described in the 'Curved Frame (saddle or 'S' shape)', Step 4 section.

First weaving using a strap.

Second weaving by hand.

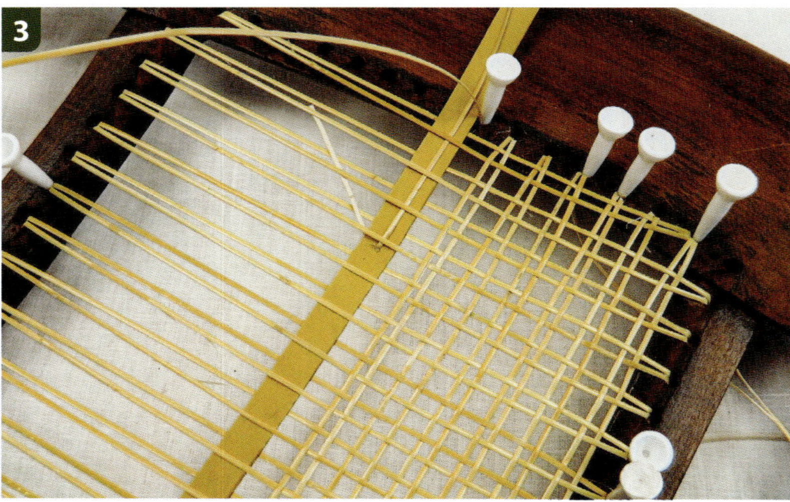


Weaving right to left using a strap.

## METHOD – DOUBLE-CURVED FRAME

This type of frame describes a shape where the curve occurs not only in one direction, as on the saddle shape, but also the other way too. The panel will have a concave curve on the horizontal and convex vertical frame uprights. These double curves are usually seen on the backs of chairs; the vertical curve hugs the back of the sitter, and creates a lumber support for the sitter's lower back. Remember to familiarise yourself with where the curves occur before you begin caning the panel; that way you can plan carefully using one of the methods described.

**Step 1** – Choose a thicker cane (4 or 5mm) and peg four or five 'foundation' canes vertically on the panel. Space them evenly from the centre. This will show the curve of the top and bottom rails. They should not be too tight and may need adjusting as the next stages go in. These canes will help keep the shape while weaving other stages, but they are temporary and will be taken out before the caning is complete.

**Step 2** – The first setting will be running horizontally; these will sit behind the foundation canes. The first setting and the foundation canes should now describe the double-curve frame shape. The key here is not to distort the foundation cane curve while still maintaining enough tension to get a vertical curve, so don't pull the first settings too tight. Please note that on certain shapes, some of the settings may also sit over the foundation canes in order to keep the curved shape consistent.

**Step 3** – Place the second setting in, following the previous stage so that you end up with a pair of settings in each side hole. The second setting can sit above the first. Go behind or in front of the foundation canes according to the curve of the frame.

**Step 4** – The weavings can now be woven vertically; you can use the steamer as previously described or just use your fingers and a bodkin. Weave in the pairs simultaneously and adjust the tension as you go, so as not to pull out the curved shapes. Remove the foundation canes as you come to them.

**Step 5** – The crossings can go in as usual; it can be helpful to weave some in both directions at the top and bottom of the panels to hold the shape. The holes can be pegged or beaded depending on the chair style.

Foundation canes for double-curved frame.

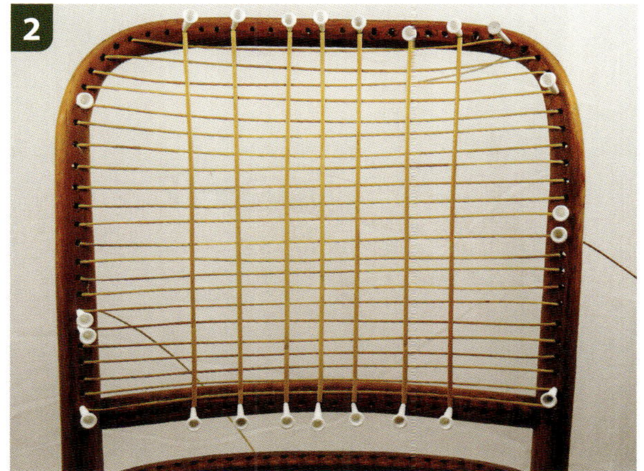


First horizontal setting.

Second horizontal setting.

First and second vertical weavings.

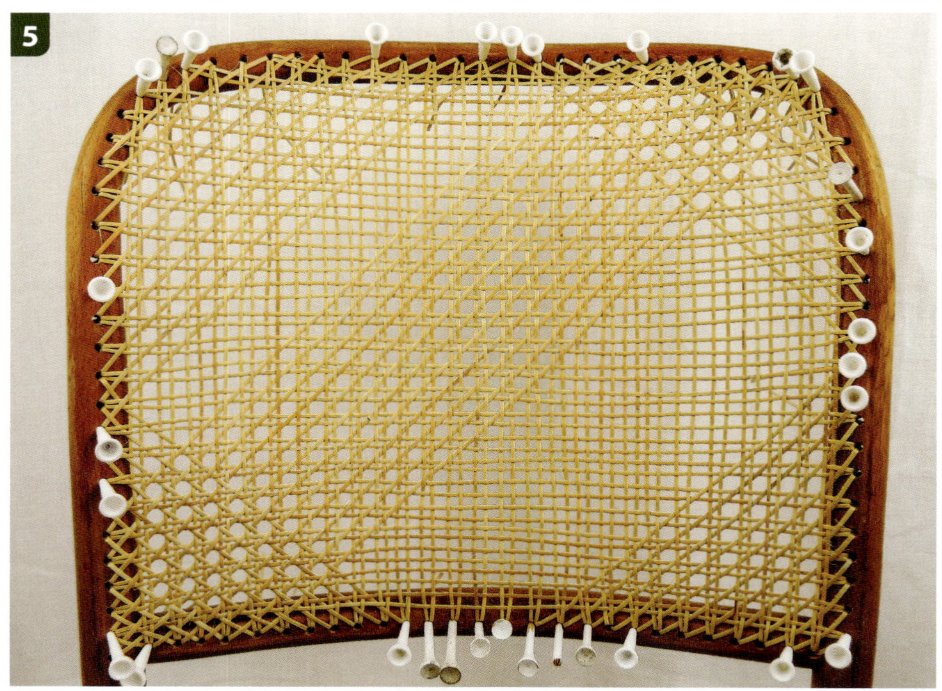


Both crossings woven simultaneously.

## METHOD – BLIND CANING

Blind caning describes cane panels where the holes in the frame are not drilled all the way through. This means there are no visible loops on the underside or back of the caning. Each piece of cane is cut to a suitable size and fixed in the blocked hole and then held with a peg. This type of caning is only used for back or arm panels as it would be unlikely to be able to take the weight of a person sitting on it if it were used for a seat. You may however have the odd blind hole on the corner of a seat frame, in the corners or where a leg block is.

Some chairs, particularly Thonet cane chairs, were originally caned in the usual way, but the back groove had been filled with a spline or fillet. These are fragile and very hard to remove so I usually cane these chairs backs blind and leave the fillet intact.

**Step 1** – To clear the old cane from a blind hole you will need to use a drill because the cane ends, and beading (if used), are usually glued into place. Test the depth of the holes using a bodkin and then mark your drill bit with some masking tape. You don't want to drill too far and then make a hole in the back! The drill should clear out all the cane and any glue in the holes.

**Step 2** – You will be following the instructions in Chapter 2 for the Standard Six-Way pattern. Make sure you have pegs or tees which are a good fit for every one of the holes, it can be frustrating if the pegs don't hold the cane securely. Put the end of the first cane into the centre hole and peg, then bring the cane across to the corresponding hole and snip the end so that there is enough to fold into the hole. Then peg and continue through the settings and weavings, pegging and then trimming the ends as you go. You can use a bodkin to fold the ends of the snipped cane before they go into the holes. I do know some chair caners like to apply glue to the cane ends at this stage – I haven't found this necessary and prefer to hold the ends with a tee until finishing off with beading or pegging.

**Step 3** – I prefer to weave the crossings in without trimming and tucking the ends of the cane. The settings and weavings will hold everything in place. You can then trim the crossing ends and place them in the frame holes as you finish. The most secure way to fix blind caning is with a peg in every hole; however, many of these types of chairs use the one peg, one beaded method or a finish with all the holes beaded. I've outlined these ways of completing blind cane panels in Chapter 3, 'Method – Beading Blind Holes'.

Fixed spline on a bentwood chair.

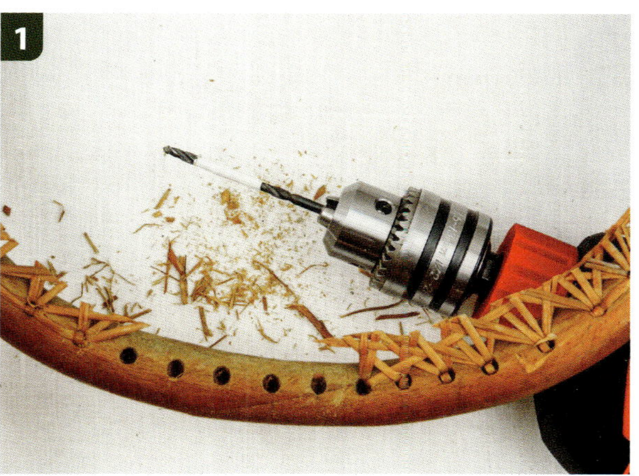


Clearing the blind holes.

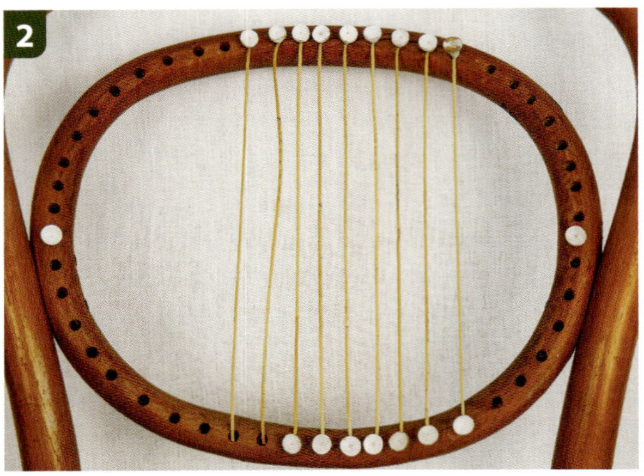

Pegs in every hole for the first setting on the blind caned panel.

Crossings with loose ends.

## METHOD – DOUBLE CANING

This type of caning can be seen on many larger pieces of furniture such as day beds and Bergère three-piece suites. Many of these types of furniture have upholstered seats and loose back cushions, or loose back and seat cushions. Some Bergère chairs have caned seats, backs and arms. Double-caned panels describe where each side of the frame is caned. It has a very elegant look; these pieces of furniture are usually more costly items due to the amount of cane work on them. These double panels are only used on the arms or backs, and mostly on the arms as a decorative device. Before you begin check if the holes go all the way through the frame, or if they are blind. I've explained how I work with both types of holes below.

**Step 1** – This method works both sides simultaneously for the crossings, which really adds to the strength of the double panel. Check that the frame holes go right through from one side to the other. Beginning on the inside of the chair, complete both settings and weavings on the inside in the usual way. Make sure that there are continuous loops on the outer side of the frame by the end of stage four; use the long tails to fill in any gaps and put a tee in any ends to hold them tight.

**Step 2** – Weave stages one, two, three and four on the outside panel, again make sure there is a loop between each hole on the other side (inside rails). For non-square or rectangles, any short ends or doubles should end in the same holes on the inside and outside panels.

**Step 3** – The crossings will be woven on the inside and outside at the same time. Start with a long piece of cane and thread it through the hole next to the top corner hole, on the inside panel. If it is an arm of a chair, I find it easier to begin on the panel in the corner furthest away from the back of the chair. Pull the cane through so half is on the outside and half the length is on the inside panel.

Thread the end on the inside through the next hole along the top rail, to the outside, then take it back through the first hole so that you have an end of cane ready to work in the same hole inside and outside.

**Step 4** – Weave the inside crossing from the top left-hand rail down towards the bottom right-hand corner. Pass the end of the cane through to the outside panel. Weave the outside cane from the top left-hand side down towards the bottom right corner. Pass the end through to the inside. It should pass through the same hole as the inside cane went through to the outside.

**Step 5** – Pass each end through the next hole along and weave the inside and outside crossings; continue until both sides have the first crossings completed. Don't forget to peg the ends – it is preferable to begin these crossings on the top rail and any ends should be along the bottom rail if possible, as this adds to the strength of the panel.

**Step 6** – The second crossings can be worked in the same way but begin in the opposite corner of the arm and work exactly as just explained.

**Step 7** – To finish, peg all the holes on the inside and separately for the outside – it is not usual to use one large peg to fill the entire hole. Cut any long tails. The loops created can serve as a beaded finish.

First side, inside setting and weavings for double caning, view from the outside.

Second side, outside setting and weavings for double caning.

Position for the start of the crossings.

First crossing on the inside panel (and showing outside crossing behind).

Almost complete first crossing on the inside panel (and showing outside crossing behind).

Almost complete second crossing on the outside panel (and showing inside second crossing behind).

Completed double-caned panel.

## METHOD – DOUBLE CANING (BLIND HOLES)

Proceed with caning each side individually as described in the 'Blind Caning' section. This will be a slow process – be careful to keep the tension on the individual strands. It really helps to use pegs which are a good fit for the holes. I usually complete the inside panel and then move on to the outside, however there isn't a practical reason for this. I like to get the slightly trickier side done first!

When you get to stages four, five, and six of the second panel you will need to employ the shell bodkin or similar tool. Part of what can make this double-blind caning difficult is that you won't have any access to the underside of the second panel. Use the shell bodkin to open the spaces where you need to weave the cane, slide the end of the cane through the space and then finish off pulling the length of cane through with your fingers. You can finish the blind panels with pegs or use the beading cane as described for blind caning in Chapter 3.

Double caned panel detail with pegs.

A tub chair with caned back and arms.

CHAPTER 5

# MEDALLION AND RISING SUN BACKS

Medallion-back chairs are also known among chair caners as 'Spider' or 'Sun Ray' chairs. All these names describe the unique style and caned pattern seen on this type of chair. The design comprises a floating wooden medallion which is usually the same shape as the chair back itself – round, square or oval. The cane work radiates outward from this medallion and holds it firmly in the centre of the caned panel. Hence the terms Spider and Sun Ray, which describe the design very well. They can be very decorative pieces and I've restored this type of chair with elaborate inlay or painting on both the medallion and chair. The Rising Sun chairs were often made during the 1930s and 40s and do have an Art Deco look. The shaped 'sun' is fixed to the chair frame, usually to the centre bottom rail or top or bottom corners. As it is a half-circle, the woven cane creates a lovely splayed sunrise pattern. I have seen these chairs caned in the Standard Six-Way pattern without taking into consideration the half sun, or sometimes the medallion pieces are not re-inserted into the chair back. It's a real shame not to copy the original design, as these chairs are so stylish and very popular.

Upholstered Rising Sun cane chair and medallion back frame.

## METHOD – MEDALLION BACK

The main preparation before you begin caning will be making sure that you position the medallion dead centre in the frame, and then making sure it doesn't move as you begin to cane, as it can get pulled one way or another as you weave in the stages of caning. I will describe a couple of ways of setting the medallion below. The caning itself does follow the Six-Way weave but there will be some changes to the usual weaving order. I have also included some finishing touches which you may come across on this type of chair, to add to the decorative style and beauty of the finished woven panel.

Before you strip the old cane away, do remember to take lots of photos and notes on the original placing of the cane, both in the frame and in the medallion. If possible, you can cut the original panel out as close to the frame as you can and hold on to it to use as a guide. I always put a bit of masking tape on the back of the medallion with a clear arrow pointing up, so I know which way it was designed to be used. You can use the hole clearer to clear the holes on the frame, but you will find that the holes on the medallion are very small – a thin, blunt nail or similar will clear these holes very well. Do take care as this part of the chair can be fragile. The holes around the medallion are sometimes blind; you will work on them as outlined in Chapter 4, 'Blind Caning'. As you begin the caning you can use your usual pegs for the frame but will need thin pegs for the medallion holes. I find matchsticks are usually a good size. You should find that there are the same number of holes around the frame as there are around the medallion.

**Step 1** – I know of three ways to stabilise the medallion in the centre of the frame before you begin the caning – whichever you use, it is essential that the medallion is held in the centre of the chair back. If it isn't, the medallion will be fixed off centre and ruin the whole effect. Keep checking with a tape measure and adjust accordingly. You will also need to check that the holes on the centre piece line up with those on the frame to create tight lines. For the first method, the medallion can be tied in place using string; place the lengths of string through the holes on the frame and corresponding medallion holes, centre top and bottom and then side to side. Knot these loops securely. You could also secure string in the corners for extra security. The medallion won't feel really fixed until you have caned the first setting, but the string will hold it at the correct height while you do this.

**Step 1a** – Use a piece of wood which is approximately 2–4cm wide, 0.5–1cm deep and 10cm longer than the chair back frame top and bottom. Using one or two small G-clamps, fix the medallion to the centre of the piece of wood, then clamp the wood to the top and bottom rails of the frame. Use some folded fabric or wood blocks between the clamps and show wood to make sure you don't mark the frame. Use a tape measure to get the correct spacing. This will hold the medallion securely in place and is a useful technique to use if the medallion holes are blind. You will need to move the wood and clamps as you cane the first setting.

**Step 1b** – This third technique won't work if the medallion holes are blind. You will need a piece of wood as described in Step 1a and four screws which are the correct diameter to go through the medallion and frame holes. Count the holes in the medallion and locate the top and bottom centre holes or left- and right-hand side centre holes if that works better for the frame. Place the medallion in the middle of the wood baton and fix it to the wood by placing a screw through the top and bottom holes. Screw these through the medallion into the wood baton. Don't go all the way down to the show wood, so that the screwhead doesn't do any damage. Locate the centre top and bottom hole or left- and right-hand side centre holes in the chair frame. Place a screw through the chair frame hole and fix the baton to the back of the chair back, through the top and bottom hole. The medallion will be held firmly in place, hopefully dead centre! This fixing could be done before you strip the cane away – you will need to clear the appropriate holes first.

**Step 2** – You will use the sizes of cane as you would for a standard seat, as described in Chapter 2; the thinner size will be used on the settings and weavings and the wider will be used for the crossings. To begin the first setting, thread a long cane 12cm through a frame hole to one side of the top centre baton (or string if using). Peg the tail, thread the cane through the corresponding hole on the medallion and then loop it through the back and bring the cane out of the next hole along. Take it back to the next frame hole and in this way work around the first side of the baton. Repeat for the second side. It is preferable to add in new pieces of cane on the frame as opposed to the medallion as this way you get the loops on the back of the medallion in place. It is difficult to trim ends on the back of the medallion. Check the loops on the back are all untwisted as these will show. Keep the tension tight.

**Step 3** – Next, weave in the second setting. Follow the layout of the first, placing the second setting to the right of the first and organising this stage so that the loops on the back of the medallion sit between

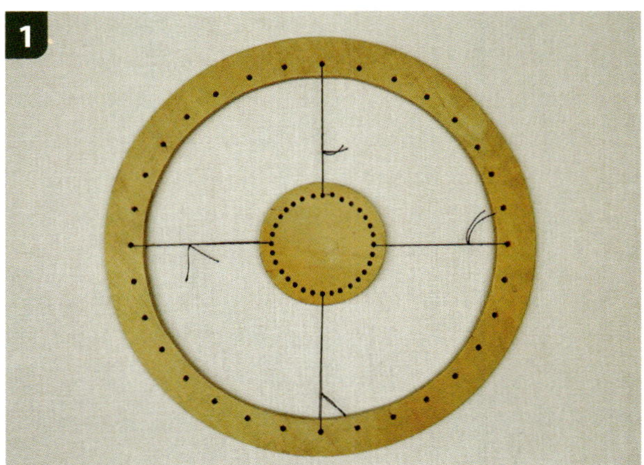

The medallion held with twine.

The medallion held to a baton with clamps.

The medallion held with baton and screws.

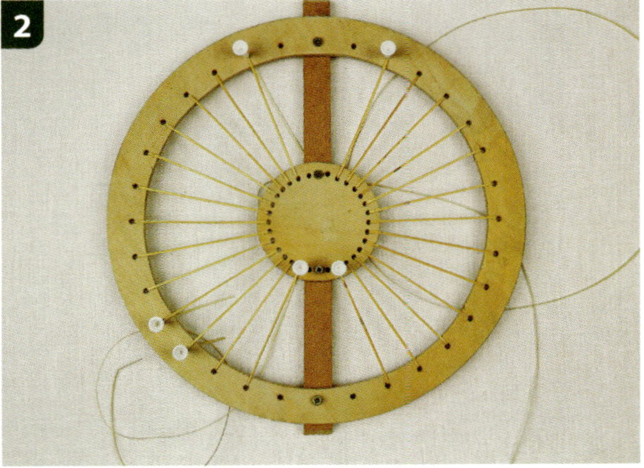

First setting on the medallion back.

Second setting on the medallion back.

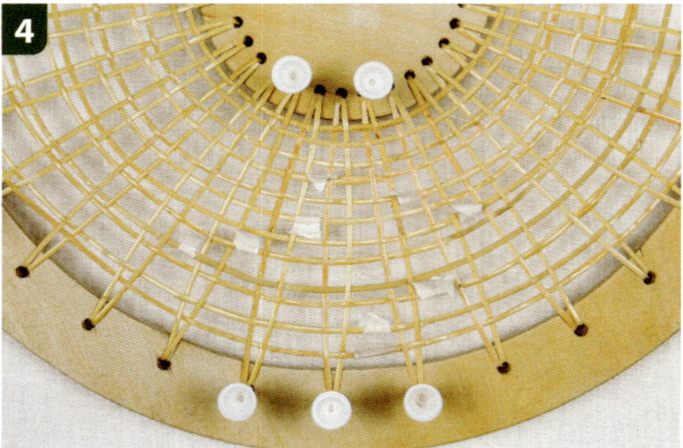
Two weavings.

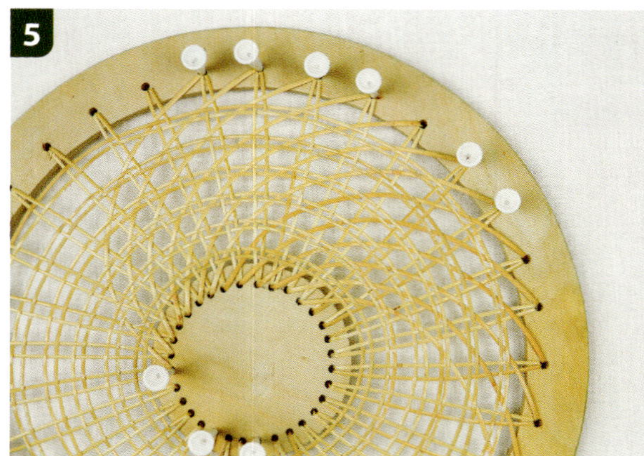
The first crossing.

the ones from the first setting. The result will be a continuous line of loops on the back of the medallion and chair frame. Once you have completed this stage, you can remove the baton (or string) and fill in the last lengths of cane.

**Step 4** – The weavings will create the circles which are such a feature of this pattern, and the rows are caned simultaneously, so the usual stages two and four from the Standard Six-Way pattern are woven in one go. Make sure you have counted the number of rings from the original panel and made a note of the distance between the medallion and first circle and the concentric circles. Use the smaller-size cane and weave under the left-hand setting and over the right-hand setting. Begin close to the medallion, cut a length of cane which will complete the circle plus tails of at least 5cm. These will be tidied up later when all the weavings are in place; they won't hold in place until more rows are in. It is useful to stagger the ends so you don't end up with joins in the same places. This can be done in the lower half of the panel and the ends can be staggered to the left and right, which should make them inconspicuous. Once the first circle is in, place in the next weaving pair, taking the cane alternately under and over the settings to the last circle, leaving the ends long where the circle joins. This is the first pair of weavings in place. Continue caning these pairs of weavings until you have the correct number of rings. Use a bodkin to adjust the distances between the rings, which very often get bigger as the rings move further away from the centre. You can then use the tails to adjust the tension of each circle and finish the ends by overlapping them around the circle, weaving them into three or four of the settings over the top of the weaving circle. I've used some masking tape to temporarily hold the ends in place.

**Step 5** – The crossings will be woven with the thicker cane size. You will be positioning the crossings as outlined in Chapter 2, however the crossings will sit in a lovely curved shape rather than the usual straight lines. If the medallion holes are not too small, weave in the cane using long strands. The first crossing goes under the weaving and over the setting (bottom left towards top right). Once you have completed the first crossings weave in the second, going over the weavings and under the settings. You may find that the holes on the medallion begin to get really jammed up after the first crossing has gone in, so use a fine bodkin to open the hole up. You can loop the cane on the back of the frame and then weave it back down to the medallion hole, trim and place the cut end into the hole. Begin with a piece of cane which is long enough to go between the frame and medallion twice plus tails. Put the end of the cane in the frame, leaving enough to loop through the next hole and weave back towards the medallion; with the first end weave towards the medallion, allowing the cane to follow the curve and then do the same with the other side of the cane piece. Press the cane ends into the small holes of the medallion, but don't come out the back as they are difficult to trim. Continue weaving the second crossings in this way.

The crossings must weave over every setting and weaving, which may mean that some go further down the sides of the frame than you may expect! Check that no crossing jumps over two pairs of settings or weavings; they must only ever weave under or over a setting and under or over a crossing.

**Step 6** – This type of panel isn't usually beaded, so trim the ends from the back of the chair frame and medallion, pegging off as described in Chapter 2 will suffice. You may want to use extra-thin centre cane for the medallion holes, or matchsticks can be just the right size. Check you have loops between each hole on the back of the frame (as the back will be seen) and the medallion; if not you can use the short ends of cane as described in Chapter 3.

The completed medallion back.

## METHOD – RISING SUN

This is a very attractive chair design. The back of the chair will have a semi-circular block either at the bottom of the chair back frame or in a corner. This block allows the settings to sit in a way which emulates the rays of a rising sun. It is good practice to photograph and make careful notes on the existing cane panel, of particular interest will be which frame holes the settings, weavings and crossings finish in and the number of weaving pairs. It may be that there is a matching number of holes in the sun block as the frame sides and top, but this may not always be the case. You could carefully cut the original panel of cane out of the frame as intact as possible; it could prove a useful guide. I usually copy the size of cane from the original and would expect that you would be using a combination of a thinner and thicker-size cane as outlined in Chapter 2.

**Step 1** – To begin weaving the first setting, first count the holes on the central semi-circular block and mark the centre with a peg. Count along the top rail and mark the centre hole with a peg. Thread a tail of cane through the centre hole on the frame and leaving a tail of 12cm, proceed to thread this through the centre hole on the centre block, go around the back and then forward through the next hole on the block. Proceed all the way along between the block and frame until you run out of holes on the block or have filled all the holes on the block and frame. It is important to note that if you have more holes on the side and top rails than on the sun block, you will need to miss some holes as you work down the side rails, as described in Chapter 2, 'Trapezium Frames'. You can judge the positions for the missed holes based on what was caned previously or by using your judgment for keeping the radiating cane settings evenly spaced. To complete the first setting, weave the other side beginning from the top centre.

**Step 2** – The next step is to put in the second setting, which uses the same size cane as the first and follows the same positions in the holes. Place the second setting to the right of the first. It is also

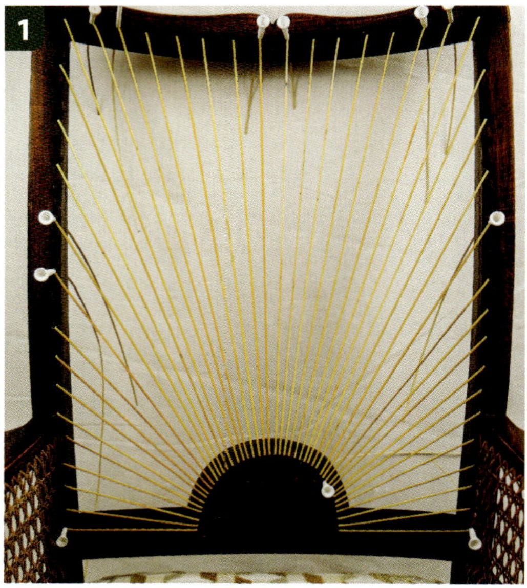


The first setting on the Rising Sun panel.

The second setting on the Rising Sun panel.

preferable to loop around the back of the blocks, in between the loops already woven with the first setting. You will end up with a loop between every hole on the back of the frame. Keep the tension tight.

**Step 3** – The weavings will use the same size cane as the settings and the pairs will be woven simultaneously. The first weaving will be placed under and over the settings and will begin in the hole in the bottom rail next to the semi-circular block, on the left, so use a piece of cane which will cover that distance plus tails. Weave around the block, under and over the settings, maintaining an even space from it and then finish in the hole directly to the right of the block. Leave 12cm tails in case you need to adjust the position on the weavings later. The next weaving (also a single strand of cane) will begin in the same hole and weave the opposite way, over and under the settings, and will finish in the same hole as the previous weaving. Continue weaving the pairs, use all the holes along the bottom rail and then move up the side rails of the panel. Keep an eye on the curved shape of the weavings and the spacing – do refer to the original panel to make sure you have the appropriate number of pairs for the panel. You will need to fill in some short corner canes at the top of the frame. These will be placed between the top and side rails on each side of the panel. Check the tension and position of the weavings at this stage as it is hard to do this after the crossings go in.

**Step 4** – For the crossings, please refer to the instruction in 'Method – Medallion Back', Step 5. If the Rising Sun block has standard-size holes, you can weave the crossings by looping them around the back of the block using a longer piece of cane. If they are tiny, just press the crossing ends into the holes. Also note that the last holes at the bottom of the semi-circular block will count as 'corner' holes so will have double crossings in them. After each stage of crossing, check the tension as you will notice that the crossings will pull the settings and weavings into position. To finish, peg the holes (*see* Step 6 from 'Method – Medallion Back').

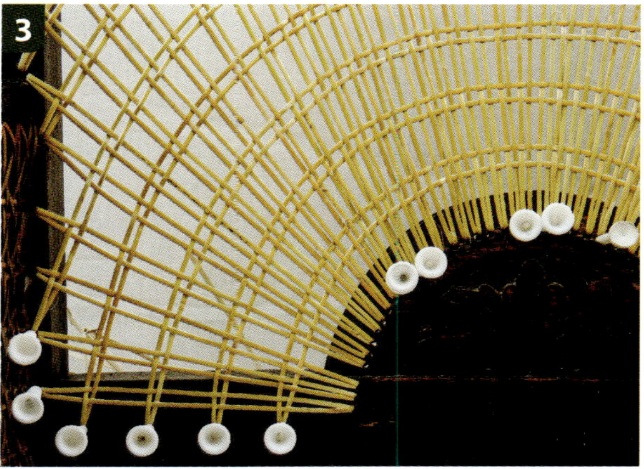

The two weavings on the Rising Sun panel.

The completed Rising Sun panel with two crossings.

## METHOD – DECORATIVE DETAILS FOR MEDALLION OR RISING SUN PANELS

These are three options for decorative detailing on this type of chair. A collar, twisted collar and an alternative way to finish the crossings. You can use all three together to really show off your skills, or a combination of the plain collar and crossing detail works very nicely.

**Collar** – This can be woven using the thinner-size cane. It is a close-caned (*see* Chapter 7) collar which you can weave using a long piece of cane, not concentric circles as described previously for the weavings. The width of the band will vary depending on the size of the chair back, but they will usually be between 1–4cm. Begin the weaving right up close to the Medallion or Rising Sun block. Leave a 12cm tail which will be trimmed at the end, and weave a single row around the block. Go under one setting, then over the next. Use the bodkin to push this up tight to the wood and then continue with the next row which will weave the opposite way to the first, over where you went under and under where you went over the settings. Continue with alternate rows until you have the desired width and finish by taking the cane end to the underside and interweave over three or four settings, do the same with the starter tail to finish. It is also possible to stagger the weave to create a twill pattern. Once the collar is in place, the weavings can all be added – *see* Step 4 for Medallion or Step 3 for the Rising Sun.

**Twisted Collar** – This will be fixed in after the collar has been completed. It will be attached around the first pair of weavings. You will need pieces of cane long enough to go around the medallion or semi-circular block plus generous tails, and the cane should be the same size as the weavings. Working clockwise, take the cane diagonally over the intersection of the setting and weaving and then under the weaving pair in the other diagonal direction. Repeat this and continue all the way around, creating a tight row. Leave the tail long for now. I have seen this type of collar left at this stage but to finish it, you will need to take the second piece of cane and weave it in the same sequence but making a diagonal cross over the setting and weaving intersection in the opposite direction to the first cane and then crossed under the weaving pair. To finish the tails, weave them into three or four of the settings overlapping the previous cane – do this on the back of the caned panel and trim them.

Collar detail.

Twisted collar detail.

**Alternative Crossings** – This style of crossings will work very well if the holes in the medallion are tight. Once the collar and twisted collar (if you are using them) are in place, use the thicker-size cane for the crossings. Put the end of the cane in the frame leaving a tail and begin the first crossing working in towards the medallion, going under the weaving and over the setting, allowing the cane to follow the curve. When you reach the last weaving which is next up from the collar, you will go under it and then take the cane back over the next setting pair along. Bring the cane under the next weaving pair along and continue weaving the crossings back to the frame hole. Finish all the first crossings. The second crossings work in the same way, but you will be going under the setting and so over the last weaving pairs. Line the loop up to fall in between the first crossing loop backs. Make sure your cane is damp for making this tight turn.

Alternative crossing technique.

CHAPTER 6

# ALTERNATIVE PATTERNS

Once you have had some experience with the Standard Six-Way pattern and the challenges of working on different shaped chairs, you may want to try out some alternative patterns. These patterns range from simple and quick, such as the Four-Way weaves, to challenging and complicated such as Star or Lace. I have illustrated the stages of weaving for all the patterns. Most of these designs are not as strong as the Standard Six-Way pattern and are only recommended for use on back or arm panels or for decorative purposes only. They will not stand the test of time on a seat, particularly one which is in regular use. However, if the seat is only lightly used, they look fantastic and are very decorative. It is also an opportunity to challenge your skills after you have become used to weaving the traditional Six-Way pattern. I have used some of these decorative patterns on doors and screens as well as chairs and they have worked very well. The next challenge would be to try inventing your own weave patterns for cane!

Various cane patterns. (Photo: Simon Booth)

## STANDARD FOUR-WAY PATTERN

There are at least two methods for weaving this super-quick pattern, probably more. Many chairs which would have originally been caned using the Six-Way pattern come into my workshop for restoration, woven with these Four-Way patterns. I often wonder if they were worked on by the itinerant chair caners working on the curbside, whose time was limited. As you can imagine because only four strands are used for these patterns, they are not the strongest, but to make up for this you could use a wider-size cane. The Single Victoria pattern is also a Four-Way weave.

**Step 1** – This is a quick process. Choose two different sizes of cane for this pattern. The setting and weaving will use the thicker cane, so the opposite to the way the different size cane is used in the Standard Six-Way pattern. Start in the centre of the frame and put in the first setting, then overlay the first weaving (as for the Standard Six-Way pattern).

**Step 2** – Use the thinner-size cane. The different directions of the crossings can go one after the other. The first set will travel from Yeovil to York, going over the weaving and under the setting; the second crossing will go in the opposite direction, over the setting and under the weaving.

Four-Way weave, first setting and weaving.

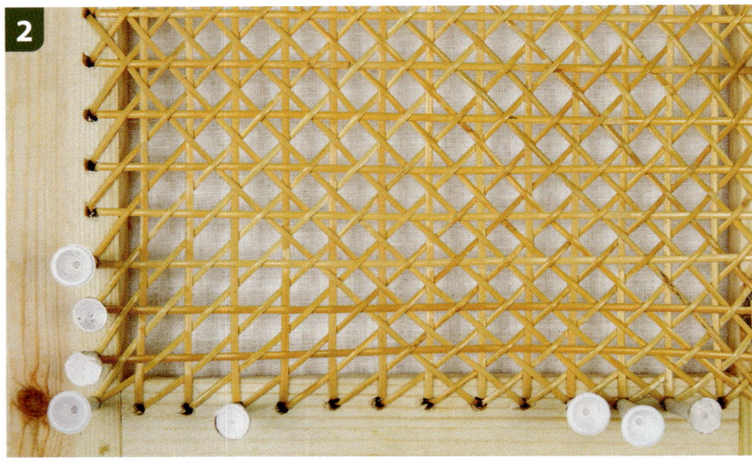


Four-Way weave crossings.

## ALTERNATIVE STANDARD FOUR-WAY PATTERN

The pattern works out the same but it is a super quick method!

**Step 1a** – Use the different size cane as for the previous method. Put in the first setting using the thicker cane size. Lay the first crossing (Yeovil to York) over the top of the setting, using the thinner cane for the crossing.

**Step 2a** – Lay the first weaving over the top of the first setting and crossing.

**Step 3a** – The second crossing lays over the weaving and the first crossing, and then under the setting and the first crossing.

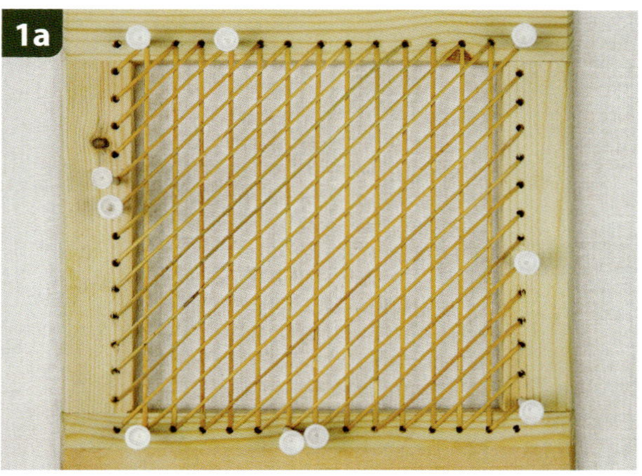


First setting and crossing.

First weaving going over the first setting and crossing.

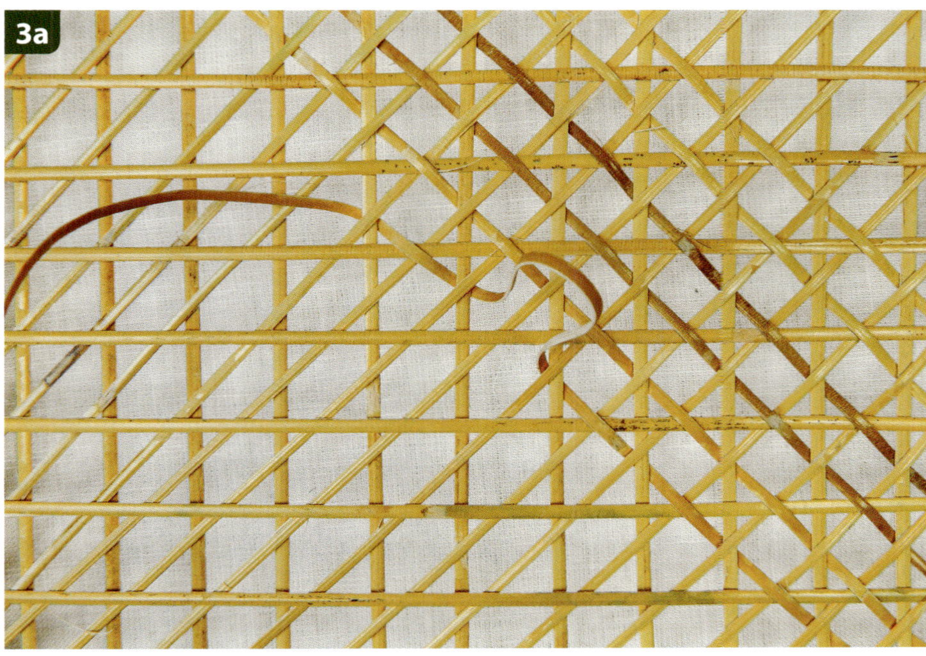


Second crossing.

## STANDARD FIVE-WAY PATTERN

The addition of the extra stage makes this pattern a bit stronger than the Four-Way pattern. Again, there are some variations. I've outlined two of them here.

**Step 1** – Use the same cane sizes as you would for a Standard Six-Way pattern, so the thinner cane for the settings and thicker-width cane for the crossings. Put a double first setting in place, so there are two canes placed in each hole. Lay the first weaving over the double setting – this will stay as a single strand.

**Step 2** – The first crossing (London to Liverpool) will use the thicker cane size and weave under both settings and over the weaving. Double up in the corners.

**Step 3** – The second crossing will go under the single weaving and over the double setting. Double up in the corners.

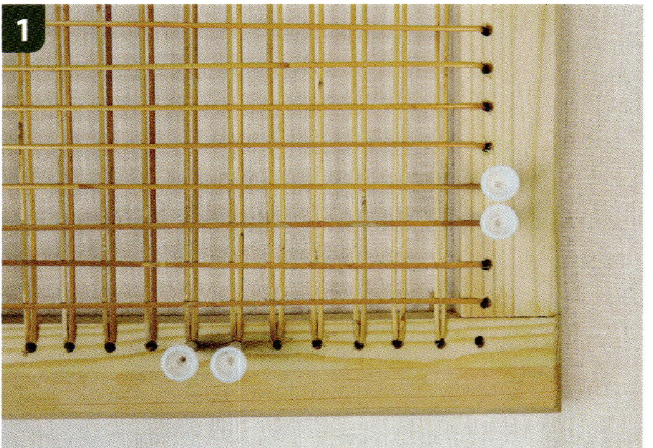

Five-Way standard pattern, double setting and single weaving.

Five-Way standard pattern, first crossing.

Complete Five-Way standard pattern, with the second crossing.

## ALTERNATIVE FIVE-WAY PATTERN

**Step 1a** – Use the thinner-size cane and put a first setting and first weaving and second setting in place, following the instruction for the Standard Six-Way pattern.

**Step 2a** – For the crossings, follow Step 2 and 3 for the Standard Five-Way pattern above.

Five-Way weave, two settings and single weaving.

Five-Way weave, completed with two crossings.

## SINGLE VICTORIA

The Single and Double Victoria patterns are very decorative. I have come across many chairs using these patterns, including furniture from India, which used very wide cane so the panel looked like a woven textile. I would recommend trying both techniques with wider cane as the pattern looks very good with the thick canes laying close together. Both these designs differ from the Standard Six-Way pattern in that the crossings sit over the intersection of the setting and weavings (not in between them). This positioning of the cane has a handy instruction – I'm not sure of the origin of 'over the bars and under the stars' but it is certainly useful!

**Step 1** – Use the same sizes of cane as you would for the Standard Six-Way pattern. Or choose a size larger if you want the end panel to look 'close caned'.

Weave in the first setting using the thicker-size cane, using every hole along the top and bottom rails, but

Single Victoria, first setting, weaving and crossing.

leave the corners free. Place the first weaving over the first setting, using every hole and the thicker-size cane. Use the thinner cane for the crossings. The first crossing (London to Liverpool) will sit over the top of both previous stages; it may not stay in place until the next crossing goes in, but it should be aiming to sit over the intersection of the setting and crossings. You only need a single cane in the corner holes for this pattern.

**Step 2** – The second crossing is the only woven stage for this pattern. Take the cane over the crossing and then under the intersection of the first three stages. Repeat this, taking the cane 'over the bars and under the stars'.

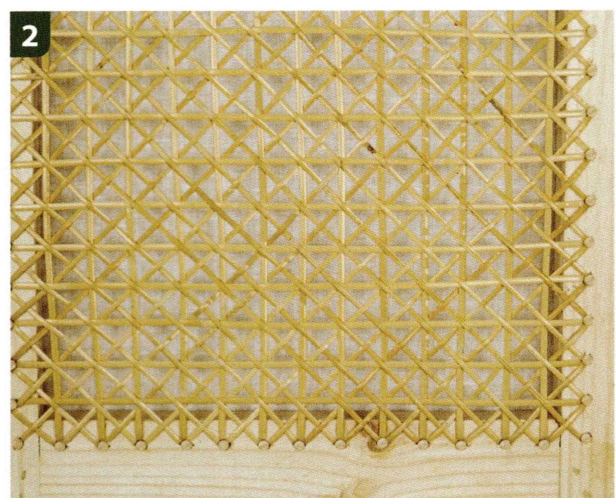

Single Victoria, second crossing.

## DOUBLE VICTORIA

The extra cane strands in the Double Victoria mean that it is a Six-Way weave using the thinner cane for the settings and weavings and the thicker width cane for the crossings. There are two other variations which make this design into a seven- and eight-step weave, outlined below.

**Step 1** – Use the thinner-size cane to put in a double setting; use every hole for the two strands of cane. Leave the corner holes free. Overlay a double weaving, two canes in each of the side rail holes. Use the thicker-size cane for the first crossing which will lay over the top of the setting and weavings, *see* Step 1 from the Single Victoria.

**Step 2** – For the second crossing, *see* Step 2 of the Single Victoria.

**Steps 3 and 4** – For a variation on the Double Victoria, you can double up either the first or the first and second crossing.

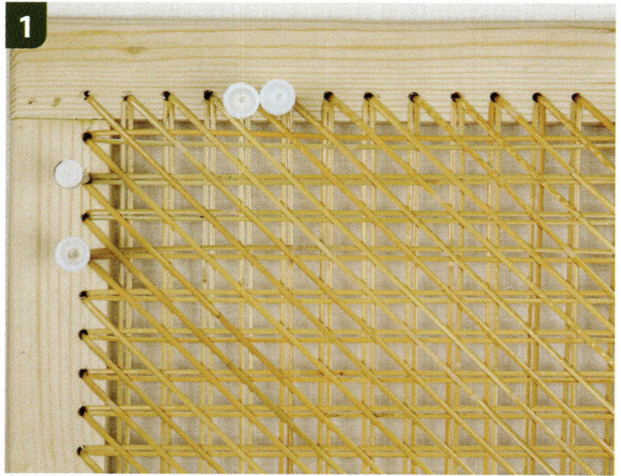

Double Victoria, double setting, double weaving, first crossing.

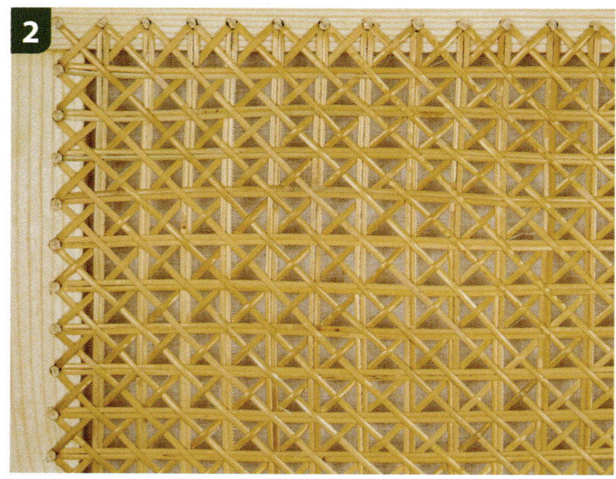

Double Victoria, second crossing.

Double Victoria, double London to Liverpool crossing.

Double Victoria, all double crossings.

## HEXAGONAL, STAR OF DAVID OR SPIDER'S WEB

The next patterns are a real step up from the standard patterns – the Star pattern has eight steps. The end results look really complicated but once broken down, you should be able to work through to completion without any problem. Due to the complexity of these patterns, it may be necessary to loop under one or two holes, on the underside of the frame, so that you don't end up having to use lots of single canes. The Hexagonal design, which is comprised of a six-pointed star, uses two different sizes of cane to highlight the star shape. This pattern is very aesthetically pleasing, but not ideal for any seats which will be in constant use.

**Step 1** – Use two sizes of cane for this pattern, weave in a first setting using the thinner cane. I'm using 2.9mm and 2.0mm. Use all the available holes, aside from the corners. Use the thicker cane for the first weaving and this will pass through every other hole on the side rails and sit over the top of the first setting.

**Step 2** – Use the thicker cane for this first of four crossings; it will go in the London to Liverpool direction and weave under the setting and over the weaving. Then miss a row of settings and weavings, so you have a crossing every other row. Work from corner to corner, across the top rail and then fill

Hexagonal weave, first setting, first weaving.

Hexagonal weave, first crossing.

in the front left corner. There will be some holes missed along the side rails, as it is important to keep the lines straight.

**Step 3** – Use the thicker cane for the second crossing. The Yeovil to York crossing will also go under the setting and over the weaving, every other row. Take the cane under the same setting as the previous crossing (Step 2), which forms a cross behind the setting. Try to finish the stage in the same frame holes as the first crossing. If the frame is trapezium, this will only work on the top and bottom rail.

**Step 4** – Use the thinner cane for the next pair of crossings. These will go into every other hole along the top and bottom rails of the frame and preferably in between the first pair of thicker crossings along the top and bottom rails. Begin with the Yeovil to York direction and keep the rows parallel to each other. Making sure the cane is damp as this can get tight, take the cane over the settings, it will go under the large crossing, Step 3 (London to Liverpool), over the large crossing, Step 4 (Yeovil to York) and over the weaving, Step 2.

**Step 5** – Use the thinner cane for this last of the four crossings; this stage will also sit in every other frame hole along the top and bottom rails, preferably finishing in the same holes as Step 4. Travelling London to Liverpool, the cane will go over the settings, over the thin crossings (Yeovil to York), under the thick crossings (Yeovil to York), over the weavings and the thick crossing (London to Liverpool).

Hexagonal weave, second crossing.

Hexagonal weave, third crossing.

Hexagonal weave, fourth crossing completed pattern.

## DAISY AND DOUBLE DAISY PATTERN

This is a very attractive design which starts with a foundation of settings and weavings from the Standard Six-Way pattern, the grid working as a foundation for the 'daisies' to weave around. This pattern works very well on square or rectangular panels.

**Step 1** – Use two sizes of cane for the settings, weavings and crossings as you would for the Six-Way pattern. Using the thinner cane, follow the instructions for the settings and weavings as described in Chapter 2. You will need to mark some of the woven intersections of the settings and weavings. You can use a pencil to make a small mark, this should rub off by the time the caning is complete. As an alternative, small pieces of string can be tied in place, or I find masking tape torn into small squares works well. They are also easy to remove. Begin with the first row of the weavings at the front of the chair frame; in the centre of this row, mark the setting and weaving intersection. Count across to the right and mark the fourth intersection along. Continue marking every fourth intersection to the edge of the frame and then fill in the left-hand side. Miss a row of weavings and mark the intersection in between the first row's markings, count four along and continue to mark every fourth intersection, every other row of weavings.

**Step 2** – Use the thicker cane for these crossings. The first crossing will travel Yeovil to York, so begin at the marked intersection closest to the front left-hand corner. Take the cane over the marked intersection, then under the weaving above and to the right. Go over the setting to the right of the previous weaving and then take the cane under the next intersection above. The cane then goes over the next pair of settings along and under the next weaving up, then over the next marked intersection. Continue with the next crossing, beginning along from where you started the previous row. However, the next crossing will begin by going under the first intersection (the opposite to the previous crossing). This stage always goes over the pairs of settings and under the pairs of weavings. You'll weave alternate intersections.

**Step 3** – This next stage will run along the same line as the previous crossing. You should finish with a pleasing interwoven crossing. Begin in the same place as before but take the cane under the marked intersection, it will go over the next setting, then under the next weaving up. You should now be at the next marked intersection, so take the cane over. It will then go under the next weaving up and over the next setting along, then under the following marked intersection. Continue for each crossing.

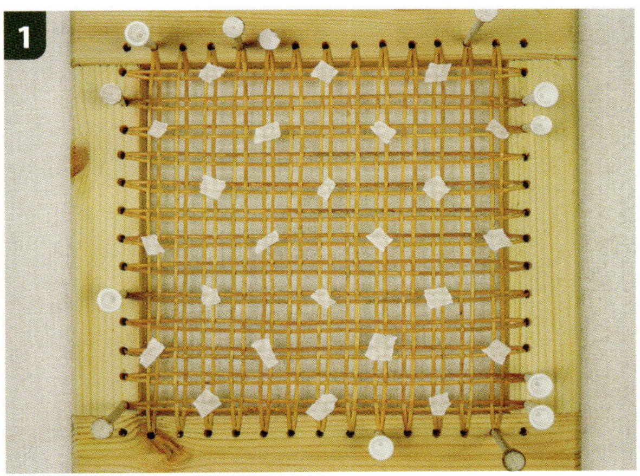


Daisy pattern, intersections marked with tape.

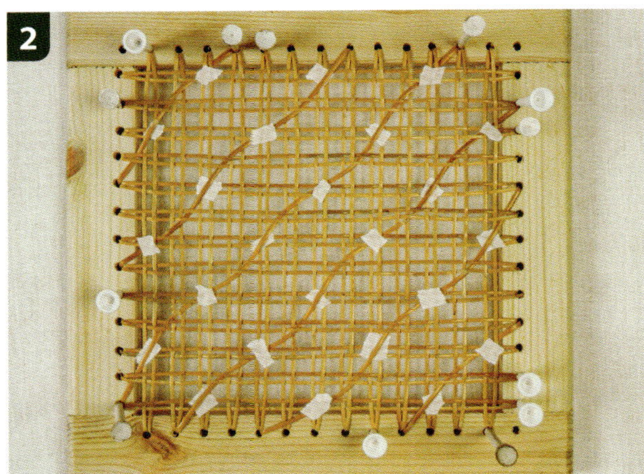


Daisy pattern, first crossing.

This stage always goes over the pairs of settings and under the weavings. You'll weave alternate intersections for each line of crossing.

**Step 4** – Use the thicker cane for this pair of crossings, which will be going in the London to Liverpool direction. Begin at the intersection closest to the front right-hand corner and take the cane under the intersection, then over the next weaving up, then under the next setting and finally over the next intersection along. Continue going over the weavings and under the settings and taking the cane under or over alternate intersections.

**Step 5** – Continue using the thicker cane for this last crossing. Begin at the same intersection closest to the right-hand corner and take the cane over the intersection (where Step 4 went under the intersection), then under the next setting along to the left. Take the cane up and over the next weaving and finally under the next intersection along. Continue going under the settings and over the weavings, going under or over alternate intersections. You can remove the markers if you've used them.

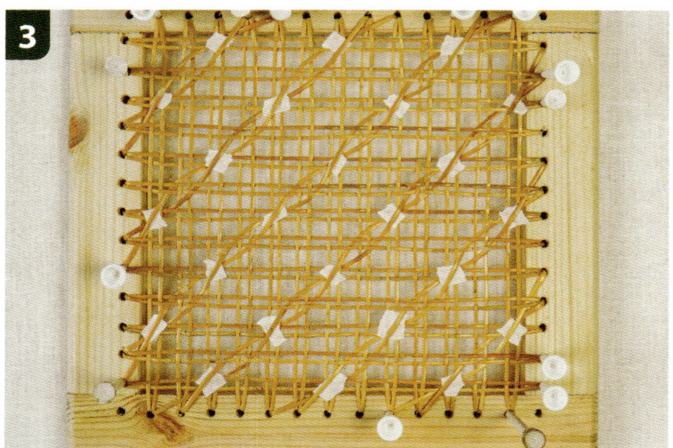

Daisy pattern, second crossing.

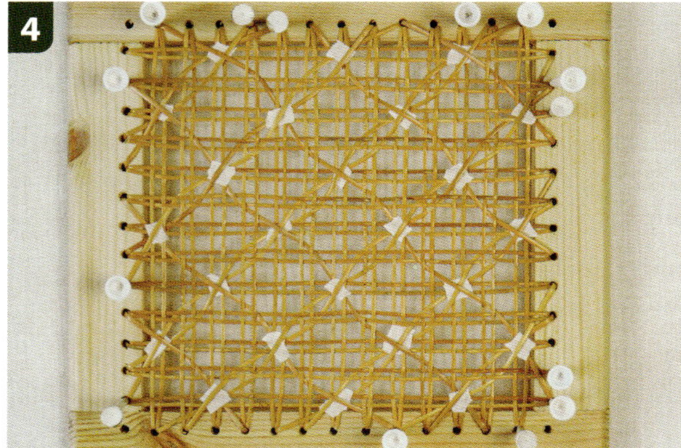

Daisy pattern, third crossing.

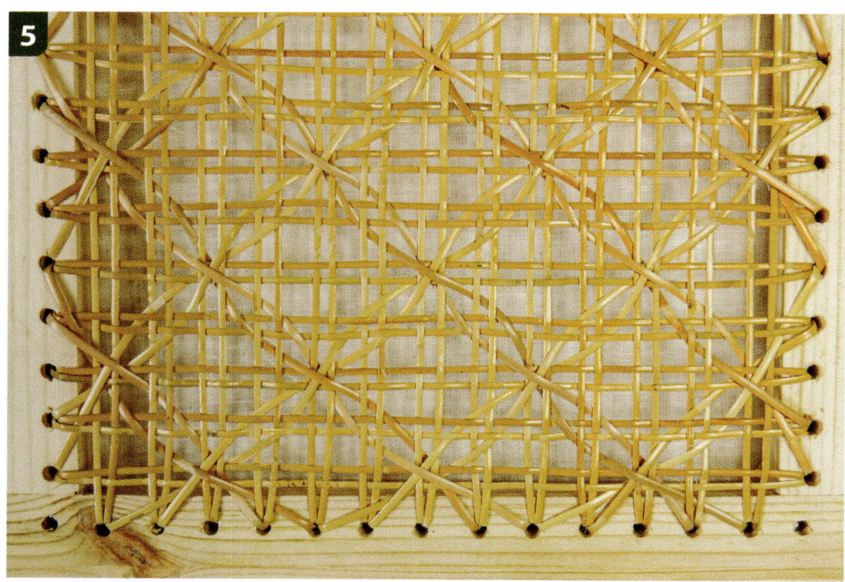

Daisy pattern, completed with fourth crossing.

## DOUBLE DAISY

This is a variation of the single Daisy pattern which doubles up the number of daisies.

**Steps 1 and 2** – Follow the previous instructions but instead of marking every fourth intersection, mark and weave every other intersection. Weave the pattern as described for Daisy, Steps 2–5.

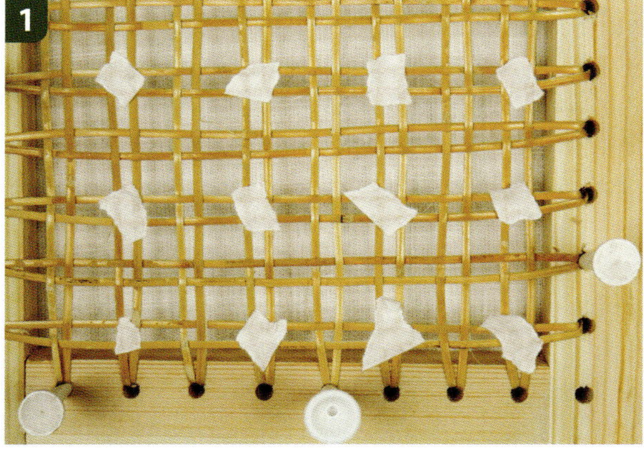

Double Daisy pattern, intersections marked with tape.

Double Daisy pattern completed.

## DAISY AND BUTTON

This is a variation of the single Daisy pattern and uses a mixture of Daisy crossings and crossings you will be familiar with from the Standard Six-Way pattern.

**Step 1** – Follow Steps 1–5 from the Daisy pattern, then weave in the crossings in both directions in the usual way as for the Standard Six-Way pattern (*see* Chapter 2). These rows of crossings sit between the daisies. Make sure the edges finish as tidily as possible.

Daisy and Button variation completed.

## STAR

This pattern has eight steps, but it is worth working through them as it's a lovely pattern. When caning the standard pattern, it is best practice for the cane to loop on the back of the chair frame between holes which are next to each other. You may need to loop under more than one hole on this pattern. Try to match the positions of canes going into the frame holes in a balanced or symmetrical way to keep the edges tidy. I have used a frame with holes which are 2.5cm apart, just to show the pattern stages clearly.

**Step 1** – You can use two sizes of cane, I've used 2.9mm and 2mm. Begin with the thicker cane. Weave in the first setting in the usual way (*see* Chapter 2, the Standard Six-Way pattern). Use the thinner cane for the first weaving, position in the usual way.

**Step 2** – This stage uses the thicker cane. The crossing will begin in the Yeovil to York direction and start in the front left-hand corner. Take the cane under two strands of the settings and then over one weaving, continue towards the top right-hand corner. Use whichever hole works best at the top, it is important to keep these crossings straight. Continue this stage, making sure that each crossing goes under the same two settings and then over the same single weaving as the first row; there is no alternation between rows. You may find that the settings push together as more crossings go in – this is fine, and the next stage will straighten them out.

**Step 3** – This second crossing stage uses the thicker cane; it will sit in the London to Liverpool direction. This strand will weave over each of the settings but under the Yeovil to York crossing which sits between the settings, then take it under the weaving and Step 2 crossing canes (where they intersect). If you are working on a square or rectangle, the ends may meet in the same frame holes as Step 2.

**Step 4** – The next two crossings are quite tight, so make sure the cane is damp and pliable. Use the thinner cane for both. You will notice the previous stages have formed a six-pointed star; you'll be weaving into the small triangles which make up this star. The first thin crossing will go in the London to Liverpool direction so begin in the front right-hand corner. Take the cane over the weavings, over the Step 2 crossings (Yeovil to York) and under the intersection of the settings and Step 3 crossings (London to Liverpool). It is important to weave only every other row of these crossings.

**Step 5** – This crossing will form a small star inside a larger six-pointed star. To achieve this, make sure

Star pattern, first setting and first weaving.

Star pattern, first crossing.

you begin the Yeovil to York crossing in the correct place. You'll be weaving every other row as for the previous stage, these rows need to line up with each other. So, begin by going over the intersection of the weaving and Step 4. Then over the thick London to Liverpool crossing and then under the intersection of the setting and the thick Yeovil to York crossing. Check to weave over all Step 4 crossings.

**Step 6** – There are two more crossing stages, also woven with the thin cane. Begin this crossing Yeovil to York and as for Step 5, locate the central star motif, take the cane over this intersection of the weaving and the crossings from Steps 4 and 5. Go under the intersection of Steps 1 and 3 (settings and thick London to Liverpool crossing), and then carry on over Step 5. This step weaves every other row where the star intersections are.

Star pattern, second crossing.

Star pattern, third crossing.

Star pattern, fourth crossing.

Star pattern, fifth crossing.

**Step 7** – This crossing is going in the London to Liverpool direction. Take the cane over the star intersection of the weaving and the three thin crossings. Then weave only taking the cane under the intersection of the setting and the thick crossing (Yeovil to York). Weave every other row, where the star intersections are. This row can feel loose so make sure you keep it pulled tight.

**Step 8** – The pattern will be looking very attractive now, but there is one more stage which balances the stars. This is a second setting and uses the thin cane. It will be going over the whole star intersection and the weavings, under the cross of Steps 2 and 3, the thick crossings. Finish by trimming the ends and peg the holes. I don't usually use beading for the decorative patterns.

Star pattern, sixth crossing.

Star pattern, the final sitting and completed pattern.

## LACE

This pattern is a variation of the previous Star design; it begins in the same way but the changes in the last two stages to produce an intricate striped pattern.

**Step 1** – Follow Steps 1–3 from the Star pattern. Cane sizes are also the same. Next this crossing follows the London to Liverpool direction and uses the thinner cane size. Take the cane over the weaving, over the Yeovil to York thick crossing, and then under the intersection of the setting and the London to Liverpool thick crossing. Weave every row.

**Step 2** – Use the thinner of the two cane sizes. This stage is a crossing travelling in the Yeovil to York direction. Take the cane over all the steps except the intersection of the first setting and the Yeovil to York thicker cane crossing. Unlike the Star pattern, weave every row available.

Lace weave foundation canes.

Lace weave with the second crossing completing the pattern.

CHAPTER 7

# CLOSE CANING

Close-caned chairs have a wonderful woven textile look to them – it is possible to weave some quite complex patterns once you have tried the basics. The chairs suitable for close caning are recognisable by two unique features. The seat will have raised show wood corner leg blocks. These support the individual strands by stopping them from sliding forward or back. The seat or back rails will also have spaced holes which look like they are designed for the usual caning, but they are too widely spaced – usually they are drilled 3–4cm apart. It is very likely that if you come across one of these chair frames, they were originally woven with willow skeins. Making willow skeins is a rarely practised craft nowadays, so often these types of chairs are woven close caned. If you should get the opportunity to learn to make willow skeins, I definitely recommend adding this technique to your seat weaving skills.

Once you have identified the frame as suitable for close caning, you will need to spend some time working on your design. I have included some step-by-step instructions for traditional twill, but you can develop your own. I find that working on squared paper is very useful for this – these patterns need to be woven in blocks of 2, 3, 4 or 5 and so on. Any smaller blocks and the cane won't sit flat or stay close. The tools and materials are just the same as for the Standard Six-Way chair caning pattern. You will need one extra tool, a 'tension stick,' which could be a piece of doweling or wood 15–20mm wide. It will need to be cut to the depth of the panel you'll be close caning. You will use only one size of cane, usually 2.4mm, 2.9mm or the 4mm beading cane.

The second style of close caning I've outlined in this chapter is seen very commonly on small Victorian folding chairs, often referred to as campaign chairs. This was because they folded and had a light woven seat and back which meant they were easy to travel with and carry while on the march. Confusingly, the close caning on these chairs is known as an Open Weave pattern, due to the spacing which this technique incorporates running down the side rails.

Two close-caned chairs; Victorian dining chair and small Victorian folding chair.

## THE LINER

The canes will be held to the frame using a small knot, which needs to be anchored by a lining of centre cane, fixed into the inside frame edge. I use 4mm centre cane for this. You will also need some masking tape and a sharp pocketknife.

**Step 1** – Cut a piece of centre cane long enough to go around all four sides of the inner edge of the frame. It is useful to soak the cane so it is pliable. Using the knife, make a long diagonal cut (a slype). This will sit on the back rail, hold it in place. Then move your hand along the centre cane to the first right-hand corner and bend the centre cane to fit inside the corner. Repeat this for all four corners and finish with a long diagonal cut which will sit flush on the first. Use some masking tape to fix the liner onto the inside of the chair frame, place the slype cut centre back, tape it and then tape on each of the other sides. The liner should be as tightly fitting as possible. Use as much tape as needed depending on the panel size. Try to avoid the tape covering the holes in the frame.

**Alternative Methods** – You can use side cutters to snip a small wedge out of each corner to help the centre cane bend into each corner. You can use panel pins to fix the liner to the frame instead of masking tape – tap them in loosely as you will need to be able to thread cane in between the chair frame and the liner.

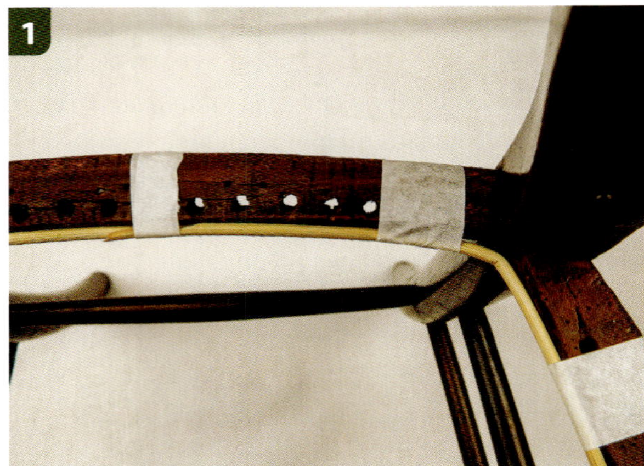

Fixing in the liner.

## THE SUPPORT CANE

This support layer of cane is also referred to as the base or foundation layer; for skeined willow seats this layer is known as the 'Johnny Save All.' Willow seats tend to break all at once so this layer of cane should stop the sitter falling through the seat. It is a nautical term which describes nets under rigging. This part of the caned panel should use cane which is wider than the size you will be using for the full woven panel.

**Step 1** – You will be caning a first setting as described in Chapter 2, using the wide-spaced holes in the chair rail. Place a horizontal weaving between the wide holes on the side rails. Weave these alternately between the settings. Trim any ends and peg the holes.

**Alternative Method** – If you have a large seat to close cane, you can make these settings and weavings into doubles; the result will look like the two settings and weavings used in the Standard Six-Way pattern as described in Chapter 2.

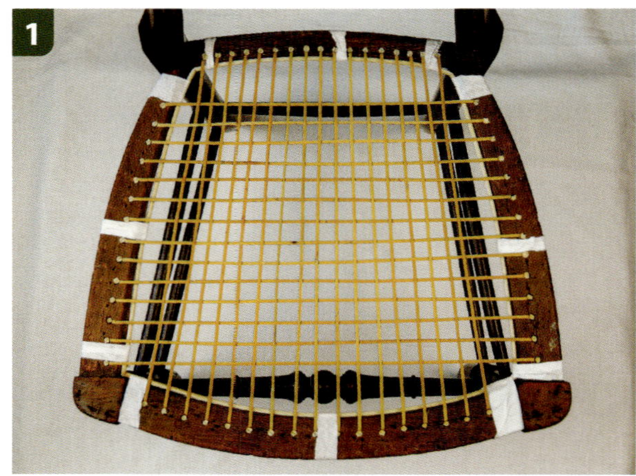

Close-cane seat support.

## THE WEFT – LEFT-HAND SIDE

Because this type of pattern looks like and is constructed in a similar way to a woven textile, I am going to refer to the two weaving stages as the warp and weft. A useful way to remember which is which is that the warp lies in the vertical direction and the weft goes horizontally from right to left (you can remember the rhyme!), but of course it also goes from left to right.

**Step 1** – To attach the weft canes, we will use a knot which interweaves around the frame and the liner. You can cut the canes to the correct size before you begin, soak them, and then wrap the canes in a damp towel. Each weft strand needs to be the full width of the frame plus 25cm extra each side. This will allow plenty for tying the knot. This stage will begin in the back left-hand corner of the frame. To begin, take a strand of the cut, seasoned cane and place a tail 5–6cm long into the corner in between the liner and the frame. Bring the long end of the cane over the frame next to the corner block. Then bring it back under the frame and the liner then over the liner and frame. Bring the end back under and thread it between the liner and the frame. This is a small wrap which will ensure that the corner of the liner is covered; ideally none of the liner will be on show.

**Step 2** – These knots will all sit on the left-hand side of the seat, all the canes will be tied on this side of the frame and then we will move on to the other side. It is a time-consuming process but I really enjoy the rhythm of the work. Take one seasoned cane and hold it approximately 25cm from the end. Place this point on the liner and wrap it over the liner and the rail. Take it under the rail, towards the back of the seat, and then bring it up and diagonally over the cane and liner. Take the end down in between the liner and frame with the end passing through the loop between the top and bottom cane. The end should thread in the direction of the back of the seat. Pull the knot in tight – you can use a bodkin to help with this. Leave the ends long underneath the rail and knot.

**Step 3** – Tie in six knotted canes on the left-hand side. I find it useful to hold the long ends on the right-hand side rail with a spring clamp. Make sure the knots are tight and pulled close to each other. As you continue, if one of the weft canes crosses one of the support canes, tie it into the knot. Note that all the caned panel will sit on top of the support canes. Also, you can remove the tape when needed.

Corner wrap.

The weft knot on the left-hand side.

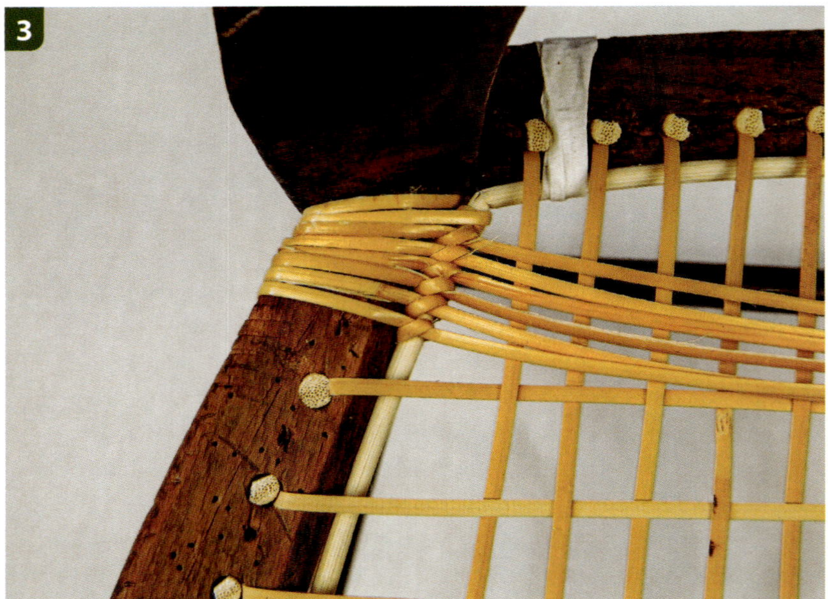

Six wefts knotted onto the rail and liner.

## THE LEADER

This type of caned panel often has a decorative woven design running along the rail sides. Not only is this decorative and attractive but it also serves the purpose of keeping all the warp and weft canes flat and in place. The leaders can be used on all four sides or just two opposite rails. There are many variations on the patterns used – some run continuously down the rails, others feature a spaced motif. I have provided instructions for a basic pattern using four strands of cane.

**Step 1** – Once you have wrapped in the top left-hand corner and tied in six weft canes, you can place the leaders into position to begin weaving them. Take four strands of cane, the same size as all the others, and place the ends of all four under the canes which have been tied into place. The canes should sit flat on the rail and side by side.

**Alternative Method** – You can use glue to stick the ends of the leaders onto the frame before you knot in the first strands, although I prefer not to use glue myself.

**Step 2** – You will be weaving the leader pattern as you tie in each of the canes, lift the two outer leaders and then knot on the four weft canes on the left-hand side. These will tie on over the two centre leaders. The outer leaders will then come down and sit over the four weft strands you've just knotted on. Lay the two outer leaders flat and then lift the two centre leaders, knot on two more weft canes, this time going over the outer leaders and under the pair of centre leaders. Continue tying on the weft canes and weaving the leader, following this pattern. Keep the knots pushed tightly back towards the left-hand back corner, using the bodkin to tighten the knots and making sure the strands are positioned tightly against each other.

**Step 3** – As you approach the end of the rail, remember the ends of all four leaders need to tuck under the last six weft canes. Try to balance the pattern so you end with the two centre leaders sitting under four knotted canes, as at the top of the rail.

Starting to weave in the leader.

The woven leader pattern.

The completed left-hand side rail with the full leader pattern.

## THE WEFT – RIGHT-HAND SIDE

You can knot the right-hand side of the weft off in blocks. Tie on 15–20 strands, weaving in the leader on the left and then repeat the process for the right-hand rail. Alternatively, you can complete the left-hand side and then approach the right-hand side in one go, as I have.

**Step 1** – Use some small clamps, masking tape or twine to attach the tension stick to the centre of the back and front rails; the weft canes must run over the top of the stick. Make sure all the cane ends to be knotted are damped down. You can turn the chair on its side, put the ends into a bowl of water then wrap them in a damp towel to keep them soft and pliable.

**Step 2** – Begin with the right-hand side corner wrap as described in Step 2, 'The Weft – Left-Hand Side'. Then bring the first strand of cane out of the damp towel, take it over the tension stick and the knot will be tied in the same way as described previously. The cane goes over the rail, then bring it back under the frame and the liner, towards the back rail, then up and forward over the liner and cane, lastly threading the end down in between the liner and the frame, towards the back rail. Pull the end to tighten the knot. This knot will be a mirror image of the other side.

**Step 3** – Carry on knotting down the right-hand side chair rail. Don't forget to weave in the leader pattern to match the left-hand side and tie in the support canes as your knots pass over them.

**Step 4** – Complete all the right-hand side knots with the leader and finish with the corner wrap at the front.

The tension stick and the cane ends wrapped in a damp cloth.

The corner wrap and first knot on the right-hand side.

The right-hand side rail weft canes with the woven-in leader.

The completed right-hand side rail.

## THE WARP

On a woven textile, the warp refers to all the yarns which run vertically. So for this stage the canes run vertically from the back rail to the front. This is the point where you will need to have your design worked out. These canes weave into the weft first and then each side is knotted off. Pay attention – it can take a few rows to get the order of the woven pattern. I have outlined instructions for a basic twill pattern, a straightforward pattern to begin with.

Don't forget to weave the leaders to match the sides if you are using them on the top and bottom rails. I begin the basic patterns in the back left-hand corner and weave across the whole panel; if you are weaving a symmetrical diamond or combination thereof, I'd recommend beginning in the centre of the panel and weave a few strands either side. This way, you can make sure you maintain the symmetry of the pattern and get it centred.

If your chair frame is trapezium or curved, you may have a space at the front and back of the knotted canes which needs to be filled in. This can be done once all the knots have been tied on to the side rails and the warp has been woven in.

**Step 1** – Make sure your canes are dampened and pliable. Cut them the width of the frame plus 25cm on each side. Begin the weaving at the back left-hand corner – you may want to turn the chair or panel side on, this twill pattern will go over four strands of cane and then under four strands. Weave the first piece of cane the full width of the panel going over four stands, then under four, over four right across the panel, leaving an even length of cane at each side. You can untape the tension stick and move it out of your way as you weave, eventually removing it completely as the panel gets tight.

**Step 2** – At the edge of the woven panel, the next strand will go over three strands then under four over four, and so on. Then the weaving sequence is:

Over two, under four, over four
Over one, under four, over four
Under four, over four
Under three, over four, under four
Under two, over four, under four
Under one, over four, under four

Then we are back to the beginning of the sequence, over four under four; repeat until the whole panel is woven. Keep the warps square, don't follow the shape of the frame if the sides are trapezium or

The first warp cane.

The twill weave sequence.

rounded. I find a shell bodkin is really helpful for lifting the weft canes on this type of weaving.

**Step 3** – Before you begin tying the knots on the back rail make sure the cane ends are damp and pliable. Begin at one end and follow the knot instructions from 'The Weft – Left-Hand Side'. It is unlikely you'll need the corner wrap as they should be covered already. Don't forget to make sure the canes are pressed right up next to each other and use the bodkin to make sure they are tight.

Once you have knotted in six canes, begin to weave the leader in, follow the same pattern and instructions from the leader section. Continue to knot in the whole rail. Don't forget to balance the leader pattern at the other end.

**Step 4** – Repeat this process for the front rail of the caned panel. If you find the tension is too tight or too slack at the end of the weaving, you can damp down the knots and then re-tie them, either tightening or loosening them where necessary.

3 The back rail warp knots.

4 The front rail knots and woven leader.

## FILLING IN

If you are working on a square or rectangle panel you won't need to do any filling in, however most chair seats are more likely to be trapezium or have curved rails. Because of this you may have gaps on the sides and front and back. These spaces will all need to be filled in.

**Side Rails 1** – It is usual for a seat to be wider at the front on the chair than the back. To fill in the side gaps left by this shape, take damp canes, and continue to weave the twill pattern until the gap is filled. Then knot off on the front rail. The other end of the cane will be threaded down into the woven panel, woven into a couple of warp canes and then trimmed. Fill in both sides.

**Back and Front Rails 2** – There won't be any available rail to knot these canes on. They should be woven according to the pattern sequence and then the ends will be threaded through to the underneath of the panel and trimmed as for the side rails.

The fill-in on the side of the caned panel.

The fill-in on the back and front of the caned panel.

## FINISHING

The last process before completing the seat is to trim all the long ends which are on the underside of the woven panel. Turn the seat over and use your side cutters or scissors to snip each end very close to the cane which is wrapped around the liner. Cut them so that you're not left with sharp points, 'dragon's teeth'!

Trimming the ends of the knotted canes.

## OTHER PATTERNS

These illustrations show designs to weave four seat patterns and two leader patterns. If you are weaving one of the symmetrical patterns, begin your warp in the centre of the wefts. It can be useful to mark the centre of the panel with some string. All the designs below are woven in blocks of two, three or four.

a. Twill.

b. Diagonal Cross.

c. Chevron.

d. Diamond.

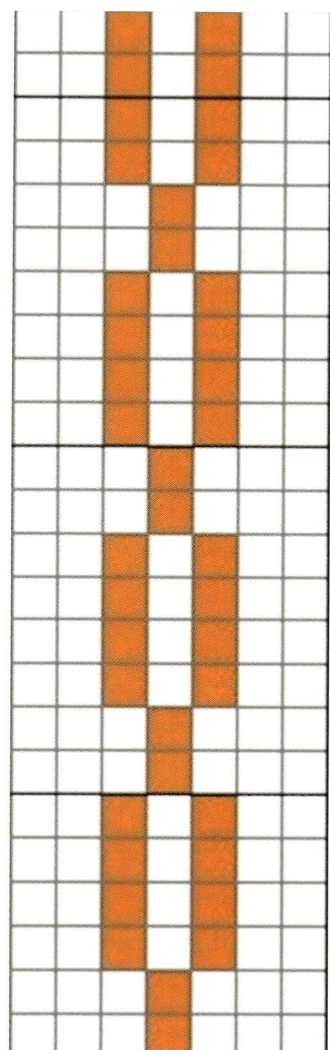

e. Leader design.

f. Leader design.

## OPEN WEAVE

This type of weave is usually seen on small folding Victorian chairs, but I have also seen this pattern used on Italian chairs designed in the 1950s. As with the close caning previously described, these are detailed lightweight decorative woven seats. I have outlined my method for weaving these panels but I'm aware there are other variations. This instruction is for when the side rails have two bindings in between each pair of warp canes, however you may find that your chair has up to four in between each pair. You can add in the relevant number of bindings according to the original chair design. If you are weaving a new panel on a chair which still has some of the original panel on it, do take lots of notes and photos so you can copy the original. A tension stick isn't required for smaller narrow panels using this method. You will need a spring clamp to hold the canes in place during the weaving process. I have left the original willow skein back panel on this chair as it didn't show any signs of damage. The new seat is woven with all 3.5mm cane.

## WEFT – METHOD

**Step 1** – Soak the cane so it is soft and pliable. Follow the instructions given in 'The Liner' and 'The Support Cane' sections at the beginning of this chapter. The smaller panels may not have the holes for the support canes. If there are no holes, then you can just fix the liner in place. I have used the original liner as it was in good condition. The unique characteristic of this type of caning is that the weft canes are double and have spaces between them which are achieved by wrapping the rails in between the weft pairs. Your measurement for each cane will need to be the width of the chair plus two rail bindings plus a 25cm tail on each side. The first weft cane will begin at the back top left-hand corner; however, to balance the pattern you will need to wrap the top of the right-hand side rail first. Take a piece of cane and thread it down between the liner and frame in the right-hand corner, take it outwards over and under the rail, wrapping the rail to cover the corner then wrap the liner and rail three times. Use a spring clamp to hold the long end in place. You can also fill in the left-hand side corner with a wrap of cane which will assure the corner is covered. Place a tail 5–6cm long into the corner in between the liner and the frame. Bring the long end of the cane over the frame next to the corner block. Then bring it back under the frame and the liner, then back up and over the frame and liner. Bring the end up and in between the liner and the frame.

**Step 2** – Use a new piece of cane, in the left-hand corner thread 1cm up in between the liner and frame (this will be wrapped in the bindings), then bring the long end from underneath up and around the outside of the frame (clockwise) around the frame and liner twice. The next wrap will go across to the right-hand side; hold the end in place with the spring clamp.

**Step 3** – Take the first cane you used on the right-hand side and use this cane end to knot in the second cane which you have just brought over from the left. The knot is as described in the Close Caning section; the cane comes under the frame and liner (clockwise) then up and over the second cane crossing towards the front panel. Finally place the end between the liner and frame and through the loop underneath, in the direction of the back rail. Pull the cane through. This will hold the first weft of the pair in place.

**Step 4** – Go back to the left-hand side and knot on over the first fixed weft strand. Use a new piece of cane, lay it over the seat panel with a tail of 25cm on the left-hand side, which wraps over the rail and

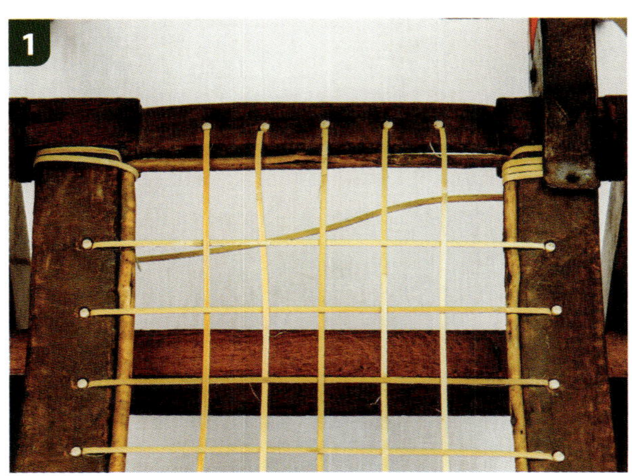


Beginning the weft corners.

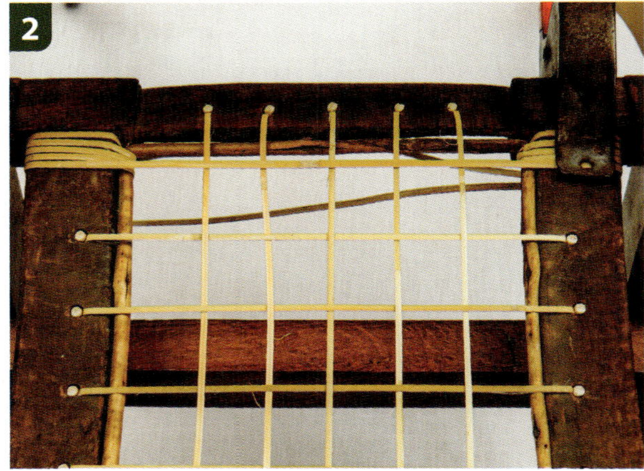


The first weft cane with a double binding.

liner, then bring the tail up towards the back rail and up and forward over the fixed weft cane. Take the tail down between the liner and frame, pass the end through and pull the knot tight, in the direction of the back rail. You can use a bodkin to make sure the knot pulls in tight. Hold the long end on the right-hand side rail with a clamp.

**Step 5** – The long end goes over to the right-hand side, bind it twice around the rail and liner, use a spring clamp to hold the bindings in place. To finish, use the long end from the previous warp strand (on the right) to knot in this second weft strand, knot as described in Step 3.

**Step 6** – Take a new cane and on the left rail, use the 25cm tail to knot in the previous weft. As this completes the pair of wefts use the longer end to bind the left rail and liner twice (clockwise). Go around a third time, then take this long end over to the right rail.

**Step 7** – You can then use the loose end from the previous two bindings on the right-hand side to knot on the new strand from the left. Then repeat this knotting process beginning from Step 4 until the whole panel has horizontal pairs of wefts with two bindings in between each pair. Keep the bindings and pairs pushed up close together and try to finish with rail bindings as opposed to a warp pair. You can also weave a leader pattern on to the side rails. Please see the instruction from the Close Caning section.

The first weft knot.

Knotting over the first weft with a new cane.

The second weft knotted on the right-hand rail with a double binding.

Left-hand side second weft pair, with a double binding.

Weft pairs with the woven leaders.

## WARP – METHOD

**Step 1** – The warp for this type of chair is usually a simple plain weave, although I have seen campaign chairs with a diamond motif in the centre of the back panel and there is no reason you couldn't try out other patterns. You will need canes which are seasoned and soft enough for weaving. Cut them to the depth of the chair panel plus at least 25cm on each side for knotting. It is usual for the warp to be woven without the spacing which was used for the weft. Begin the weaving at the back left-hand corner – you may want to turn the chair or panel side on. The plain weave pattern will take the first cane over one pair of wefts and then under the next pair. Alternate each warp cane, so the next one will begin by going under the first weft pair. Weave the full width of the panel using this under and over process and leave an even length of excess cane at each side. If you have a trapezium-shape chair run the first piece straight, so it will sit tight in the back-left corner but there will be a space between the front-left corner and the cane strand. You can fill the sides in once the central panel has been woven in and knotted. If it is a small panel, I prefer to knot off the front and back rails in one go but you can knot a section of six or so at a time if you prefer. Begin with the back rail and follow the instruction for the knot in Step 1, 'The Weft – Left-Hand Side'. Make sure the cane ends have been soaked and are soft and pliable. You can dip them in water and then wrap them in a damp towel. Don't forget to weave in the leader pattern if you are using one (*see* 'The Leader' section earlier in this chapter). On the chair in the illustration, I have copied the central motif from the original back panel.

**Step 2** – Knot the front rails so that the knot sits in the same direction as the back rail. Weave in the leader.

**Step 3** – If you have a round or trapezium panel you can now fill in the sides where needed (described in the previous Close Caning section). Once all the knots are in and the fill-ins woven, you can turn the panel over and trim the ends as described in the Close Caning section.

Knotted-on warps with the leader motif.

The front rail warp knots.

The completed panel.

CHAPTER 8

# BINDER CANE

Binder cane is often referred to as lapping cane. It is a wide cane, 5–6mm, and can be used to wrap or 'lap' joins on garden furniture as well as weaving cane panels for seats or backs of chairs.

It is available to buy with a glossy side (the same as the cane we have used up to now), or matt. The types of seats this is used for only ever use the glossy cane.

In this chapter I'll be outlining how to use this wide glossy cane to weave strong seats or backs of chairs. The use of this type of cane was popularised during the 1950s and 1960s in Scandinavia. Well-known designers such as Hans Wegner used this material on some of the most iconic chairs of the time. The PP01 chair, known as 'The Chair', is one of the most famous of his designs and has a wonderfully decorative woven seat. In my experience of restoring these types of chairs, most of these high-spec designed chairs have their own woven detailing, which makes each chair unique. I am going to outline the instructions for weaving a basic binder cane pattern, such as would be seen on the 'Cow Horn' chair PP505, designed by Hans Wegner. The chair frame I'm using is a No.75 dining chair designed by Niels Moller – it would usually be seen with a paper cord seat.

The method will use single pieces of binder cane cut to size and then woven into a close-caned seat or back. Once you are familiar with the method, you can add in the extra detailing which may be unique to whichever chair you are restoring. Always take lots of photos and unwrap the old cane so you can see how it was originally woven and fixed. This weave has double warp and weft pairs; this is known as a Basket Weave (over two, under two). It will also incorporate a leader as described in Chapter 7. Of course, you could weave this type of seat onto any suitable frame. The chair would need to have front leg corner blocks, and no holes in the frame are required. The warp and weft use fine tacks to attach them to the frame, but each has its own variation on the binding and fixing method. You may find some chairs you work on only use one of the methods described.

You will need some extra tools for this technique; a light hammer, fine steel tacks, a spring clamp, a pencil and a pin drill. This is a small handheld drill which uses micro-size drill bits. One of the trickier parts of working with the binder cane is that it needs to be tacked onto the wooden rails. If you tack the cane straight onto the rail you will most likely find that it splits, which can be the source of much frustration. I use the pin drill with a 1–1.5mm drill bit

Danish dining chair with binder cane seat.

to drill a hole into the ends of the cane before I use the fine tack to attach it to the rail. This may seem time consuming, but it really works – you'll definitely spend less time having to replace split canes!

To finish the underneath of the woven cane panel, you will need to cover all the tack heads. For this I use a type of cane called Kooboo, which is round, like centre cane. This type of rattan was commonly used for making school canes. You may have seen these with a bent end to make a handle, luckily not a common sight in schools anymore; they must have really hurt!

## THE WARP

Choose which size cane you are going to use, either the 5 or 6mm. I am using 5mm in the example. This decision should be based on the original if you are restoring a seat or according to your personal preference if it is a new piece. The wide cane is very thick and will break easily, so needs to be well soaked, at least 20 minutes in warm water. You could leave it in the water while you work. As the thick cane dries out, it will mould into whatever shape it has been placed in. The warps will run in pairs, with one or two wraps around the rail in between each pair to space them out. This is so there is enough room to weave in the weft canes. Use a spring clamp at any point you need to hold strands in place before fixing. You will need an odd number of warp pairs so mark the centre of the front and back rail – there will be a warp pair on the centre line.

**Step 1** – Cut the cane to sized lengths for the warp. You will need to use a tape measure to calculate two or three bindings around the frame, added to the depth of the seat from front to back. Add an extra 20cm for pulling and fixing. Make sure the cane is soaked as described above so it is soft and flexible. Mark the centre point of the front and back rails with a pencil. To accommodate the trapezium shape you will need to utilise more bindings on the front rail than on the back rail. You can add in extra bindings as you work. If you are working on a square, you will use the same quantity of bindings on the front and back rails. Take your first piece of soaked cane, then using the pin drill and a 1mm drill bit, drill a small hole approximately 1cm from one end. The illustration shows a practice piece tacked onto some spare wood.

Drilling a hole in the cane with a pin drill and a tacked-down cane.

First warp cane attached to the inside front rail.

**Step 2** – Hold the short end of the cane against the inside front left-hand corner of the frame and tack the first cane in place. You will have the long length of cane hanging down from this point. I have also marked a guide tack line on the inside of the rail.

**Step 3** – Take the long end of the cane under the front rail, then up and over the top. Bring it over to the back rail, hold it in place with a clip. Mark with a pencil where the tack needs to go in to attach the cane to the inside of the back left-hand side rail. Drill the hole with the pin drill and then trim the cane 1cm from the hole. Hold it in place and tack the cane down.

**Step 4** – Take another piece of soaked cane; this will be the second of this pair of warps. Tack it off in the same way as in Step 2, on the inside of the front rail next to the previous piece. The long end will be hanging below the frame. Take this under the front rail then up and over so it goes across to the back rail. This time you will bind the cane around the back rail once. Then, tack the end off as described in Step 3. This is the first pair of warps in place. You will also have a single binding on the back rail.

**Step 5** – Use a new piece of cane and begin by tacking off the short end on to the inside front rail, take the long end of the cane under then around and over the front rail, bind it twice. Take it to the back rail. If you have a trapezium frame you will have double bindings on the front rail and singles on the back. This is so that when you reach the marked centre point, the warp pair lines up squarely. You may only need to use the single wraps on the back rail a few times. It is best to do them close to the corners of the panel on the back rail. Tack the end of this cane without binding it, fixing it onto the inside of the back rail.

**Step 6** – Repeat Step 4. You will now have two pairs of warps, with a single binding on the back rail. As more tacks go in, follow the line marked on the inside of the frame to keep them in a straight line.

**Step 7** – You can now begin to weave the leader onto the front and back rails. This chair will only have these woven into the warp pairs, there isn't usually a leader woven into the weft. The leader should sit over the warp pairs and underneath the rail bindings. You can use one or two strands; this will depend on how wide the rails are. I have woven in one cane on this example. On the front rails, take the cane over the pair of warps which were just fixed in place and then press the end of the leader under the first four canes next to the corner. Do the same on the back, but go under the first three canes.

Cane tacked down on the left-hand side of the back rail.

The first pair of warps with a double binding.

**Step 8** – Repeat this sequence until you reach the centre marks on the rails. It is important that you have a warp pair sitting dead centre, so that you get an odd number of warps. The pattern won't balance if you have an even number. You can double the bindings on the back rail once the distance to the centre point measures the same as it does on the front rail. Continue with the right-hand side of the centre points. When the warp stage is complete, the sides of the centre point should mirror each other in terms of warp pairs and binding numbers. The leader will also finish by tucking under the last four strands of cane on the front and under the last three on the back rails.

**Step 9** – The underside of the front and back rails will show as two bindings and two tacked ends.

A double binding and single warp cane.

The second pair of warps attached to the back rail.

The leader on the back rail.

The completed warps.

The warps fixed underneath the back rail.

## THE WEFT

The weft cane will be the same size as the warp, I'm using 5mm. These types of seats always use the same size for the warp and weft. The weft is woven without a leader and the tack will sit on the top of the rail, as opposed to on the inside as we did for the warp. I am demonstrating two methods of fixing the canes onto the rails in this project, you will then have both techniques to use for whichever chair design you are working on. To complete the Basket Weave pattern, the weft canes must be woven in pairs, same as the warp.

If it helps, use a spring clamp to hold the cane in place at any stage that you need to.

**Step 1** – Cut lengths of binder cane. These need to be the width of the frame, plus a wrap each side and 20cm for holding and pulling. Make sure the lengths have been thoroughly soaked in warm water. Begin in the back left-hand corner of the frame. Bring the end of the cane up from underneath the panel in between the warp pairs and the inside edge of the frame. You are going to take this end up onto the top of the rail and fix it off there. Mark a spot on

The first weft tacked down on the left-hand side rail.

The first weft fixed on the right-hand side rail.

the cane 1cm from the end and use the pin drill to make a hole. Tack this end of the cane off, lining the tack up with the centre of the top of the rail. You will have the long end hanging underneath the panel. Bring this around the rail clockwise and up and over the top of the tacked-off end.

**Step 2** – Take the long end over the first pair of warps and weave under and over the pairs until you have woven all the warps alternately. Don't weave in between the close pairs of canes, treat them as one, going over both or under both. As you have an odd number of warp pairs you should finish by going over the last pair of warps in the back right-hand side. To fix the weft cane on the right-hand side, bring it all the way around the right-hand side rail and then up in between the warp pairs and the frame onto the top of the rail. It will need to come forward and sit on the top of the rail, next to the loop which just went around the frame. Make sure the weaving is tight and then mark the point you want to tack with a pencil. Use the pin drill to make a hole and then tack off. Use a knife or sidecutters to trim any excess cane 1cm from the tack.

**Step 3** – For the second of this weft pair go back to the left-hand rail and fix the cane strand as described in Step 2. Weave the strand in, following the same pattern as the previous cane. Make sure the cane is tight and then bring the long end over the tacked-off end of the previous strand, bring it up in between the warp pairs and rail, place it next to the cane you just wrapped and then mark with a pencil, drill the hole, and tack off.

**Step 4** – Continue weaving the weft pairs in the same way; you will need to alternate the pairs as they weave under and over the warp pairs. Fill the whole panel. Make sure the weft canes are sitting as closely together as possible. Your last weft will need to tack off on the inside of the rail (same as for the warps) as you will have run out of rail space on the top.

**Step 5** – To finish, you will need to use the Kooboo cane to cover the tacks where you fixed off the warp pairs. This really helps to keep all the canes in place, and also stops the cane ends from splitting around the tack holes. The Kooboo cane comes in various sizes so choose one that is appropriate for the size of panel you are weaving on; I have used 4–6mm on this example. Use a sharp knife to carefully split the cane in half, then ease the cane apart with the blade. Once it is split, trim it to a length which matches the inside warp rails and use the pin drill to drill tack holes every 7–8cm. Begin 1.5–2cm from each end so the tips can be fixed down properly.

**Step 6** – Tack the Kooboo cane strips on to the inside frame to cover the tacks which are holding the warp canes in place. Trim the ends of the cane so they don't show.

The second weft tacked down on the right-hand side rail.

The completed seat.

Splitting the kooboo cane.

The tacked-down kooboo cane.

CHAPTER 9

# REPAIRS AND DYES

As you begin to work on more caned chairs, you will notice the many sizes and styles available. From a simple occasional wooden-framed Victorian dining chair to wonderful large daybeds and three-piece Bergère suites, the variety is huge. Caning a whole new panel on some of the larger items may seem daunting but as you gain confidence on smaller projects, you will soon feel capable of tackling a substantially sized piece. Bergère suites are relatively common, usually a sofa and two matching armchairs often with highly elaborate and attractive carved frames, cane arms and back panels (sometimes the arm panels are double caned). They are usually luxuriously upholstered seats plus feather cushions. Very often these larger pieces which have backs and arms will have some original panels intact, and some panels with breaks or holes; it is possible to repair these small breaks as opposed to weaving whole new panels. Please note however that you can repair backs and arms but never a seat – unless the seat is never going to be sat on! The backs and arms take a lot less pressure than a seat, so a repair in the cane will hold. The pressure which a seat is put under means a patched repair would never hold. The new cane patch will simply push through, and the original canes will continue to break around the new woven area. This method of repairing the cane panels is called splicing. It can be fiddly, and some patience is required, but splicing some new cane into existing areas is a good way of repairing without having to replace a whole panel.

This chapter also covers tinting new cane. If you are adding new spliced patches to existing panels, you will often want to dye the new canes to match the original material. I've outlined which dyes and pigments I use to do this. These colouring methods can also be used on completely new panels, which is useful if you are caning one seat from a set, for example. The cane already has a naturally protective shiny surface which does repel wood dyes, so the colour will be many shades lighter than the true dye colour. You will need to try different colours to see what shade is achieved on the finished panel. The true dye colour will show on the absorbent underside of the cane.

Cane panels, dyes and brushes.

## REPAIRS – SPLICING

Before you begin to weave in a spliced patch, you will need to assess the whole panel and judge whether it is just one small area which needs a patch or several places. If there are several places, assess each of them – it might be more suitable to remove all the old cane and weave a whole new panel. If the cane hole is at the edge of the frame, you may need to clear some of the old pegs out of the frame holes. Once the new splice is woven and trimmed, you can choose to dye it to match the existing cane colour. You could also consider leaving it in the natural colour; this celebrates the life story of the chair, and this type of 'visible mending' is a popular approach for a sympathetic restoration.

**Step 1** – To begin, you will need to ascertain the correct size of canes which have been used on the original panel. If it's not clear, hold up some new cane next to the original and match the size visually. Next you will need to trim away all ends which are hanging loose, which may make the hole a little bigger, but you need the loose ends out of the way. Once you have done this you can dampen down the edges very lightly with a cloth or sponge. This should help the new canes to thread into the original cane. If the hole is next to the frame edge, you may also need to trim the beading back if it's also broken and clear any pegs from the frame holes for the new canes to thread into.

**Step 2** – I like to begin weaving in the canes in the usual order for the Six-Way pattern, so soak some cane for the settings and weavings. Cut these to the size needed plus about 20cm each end. Take the first cane and weave in the settings, begin the weaving approximately 2cm before the panel hole, going over the existing original cane, and finish 2cm past the panel hole. At this stage, leave the ends long and continue to weave in all the missing setting canes. Take the new cane strands to the frame edge and into the frame holes if needed. You will find a fine bodkin really helps to open some space for the new canes to pass in and out. Complete all the new weavings in this way, making sure you weave the pattern the same as the rest of the panel. Thread the tails into the frame holes if needed.

Preparation for splicing a patch.

Spliced setting and weavings.

**Step 3** – Change the size of cane if needed and complete caning in the crossings as described for the settings and weavings.

**Step 4** – Use some sharp side cutters to trim all the ends of the new cane. Trim as close to the point where they meet the original cane as possible. On the crossings, make sure the trimmed edge is at an angle so it's hidden. Use some centre cane to peg any frame holes, and weave new beading into the existing cane beading strip if your chair has beading. You can now dye the new cane to match the original.

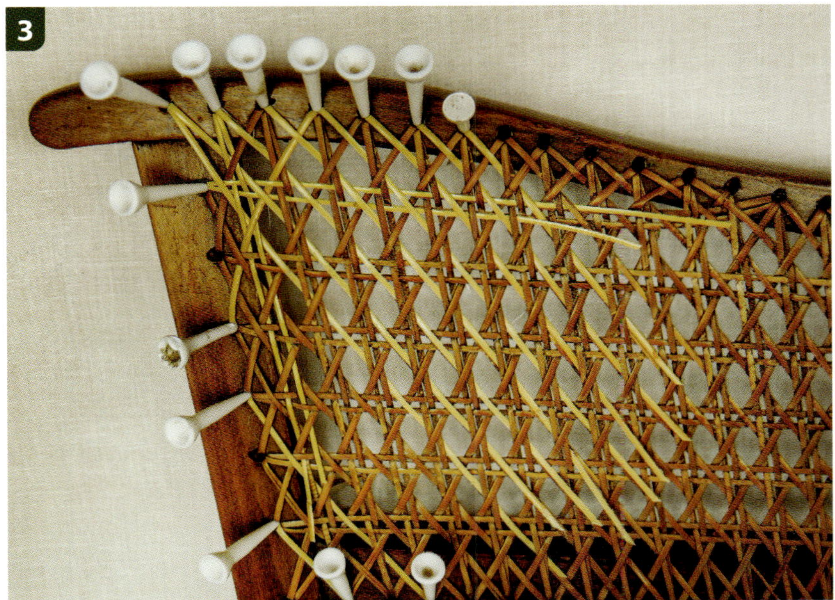


Spliced crossings.

Completed splice with pegs.

## DYES FOR CANE

I really like the natural colour of new cane. I would usually leave a new panel untreated and let time take its course, as it will eventually darken to a rich gold if left to its own devices. One of the joys of working with plant-based materials is that they carry on changing over time. The dyes and colours don't add to the strength of the cane and are used for cosmetic effect. Having said that, I'm not aware that any of the finishes will damage or limit the lifespan of the cane seat. If you need to, you can mix colours to match an original colour, which will be useful if the chair is part of a set and you are only caning one seat. As I mentioned in the introduction, whichever types of dyes, pigments or polishes you use on your cane panels you won't achieve the true colour of the dye. The shiny side of the cane will repel the colour and only a light wash colour can be achieved. Because of this it's a good idea to trial colours before applying them to the cane. You can buy pre-woven sheets of cane and I find them very useful for working on colour matches.

Do allow plenty of time for the dyes to dry, and test that none of the colour rubs off as this could be difficult if the chair is in regular use. No preparation is needed on the cane before applying any of the colour treatments listed below. You may want to wear gloves.

**Spirit wood dye** – I prefer the spirit-based dyes to the water-based wood ones, the newly woven cane seat will absorb the water-based dye and go very wobbly and soft. Luckily, it will dry out nice and tight again, but it can be worrying! You can buy sprit-based wood dyes from most hardware shops or online suppliers; they usually have a selection of shades available. You can apply as many coats as needed, let each one dry before applying the next. Apply to the top shiny surface of the cane with a soft paint brush. I never apply any dyes to the absorbent underside of the cane, I think the cane needs to breathe and keep its elasticity – if the underside was coated in dye, it may go brittle. Some dye will always leach to the underneath but this is nothing to worry about.

**Powder pigments and shellac** – I use this type of colour if the canes need to be very dark. You will need some shellac polish, some powder earth pigments and methylated spirits. All these items are available from hardware shops, or you could

Spirit wood dye.

Powder pigment and shellac.

contact a wood polish specialist supplier. The earth pigments are natural powder pigments and give lovely rich colours. These can be mixed with some methylated spirits and shellac to give a rich shade. You can mix the meths to shellac, two parts shellac, one part meths. I would recommend using a jar and measuring this mix out, then you can add the powder pigments incrementally, maybe half a teaspoon at a time, until you get the desired shade. If you run out, you can then mix the exact same colour again using the same measurements. Do test the colour first to make sure it is the right shade. You can apply it smoothly and evenly with a small, soft paint brush. French polishers use a rubber which holds a lot of polish, but a paint brush will suffice for a smallish seat area. Work the colour into all the crevices and areas where the canes cross, leave to dry overnight. This type of dye is ideal for colouring smaller spliced patches.

**Van Dyke crystals** – These are made from crushed walnut husks and were traditionally used for dying oak, walnut and mahogany furniture. They are water soluble, and these are the only water-based dyes I'd recommend because the colour is so good. You will need to measure out a quantity of hot water and add the crystals a teaspoon (or other measurement) at a time until you have the desired colour. A guide would be 100g of Van Dyke crystals to 1 litre of water. Don't forget to make a note of the mix quantities in case you run out of dye and need to mix some more. Test the colour on some sheet cane and then apply to the cane work with a brush. Leave to dry overnight. This will also make a good colour for a spliced patch.

**Paint** – I am not a huge fan of painted furniture as I think wood and cane have such lovely natural qualities, however a great deal of caned furniture is lacquered, japanned or painted so it's good to know that you can paint the cane work if needed. I recommend using eggshell paint and applying it to the cane with a small paint brush, making sure it gets into all the areas where the canes cross and the beading. Take care where the cane lies on the chair frame, you may need to use an ear bud or similar to remove the paint from the frame in these areas. Leave to dry for 24 hours.

Van Dyke crystals.

Eggshell paint.

# FURTHER INFORMATION

## SUPPLIERS

Cane Store
www.canestore.co.uk
Mill Farm
Mill Lane
Crewe
Cheshire
CW2 5NX

Seatweaving Supplies
www.seatweavingsupplies.co.uk
210 Station Road
West Moors
Ferndown
Dorset
BH22 0JD

## FURTHER READING

Holdstock, Ricky,
*Seat Weaving*, Guild of Master Craftsman Publications Ltd 1993

Miller, Bruce W. & Widess, Jim,
*The Caner's Handbook*, Lark Books 1991

Johnson, Kay;
Elton Barrett, Olivia;
Butcher, Mary,
*Chair Seating*, Dryad Press Ltd 1988

Dunwell, J. & Kingdom, M.
*Chair Caning Methods for Frames of All Types*,
Self-Published, J. Dunwell 1969

Brown, Margery,
*Cane and Rush Seating*, BT Batsford Ltd 1976

Maynard, Barbara,
*Cane Seating*,
Dryad Press Leaflet 513, Dryad Press 1977

Peterka, John & Lillian,
*Ideas for the Experienced Caner*, Self-Published,
Peterkas 1977

# GLOSSARY

**Settings** – The vertical strands of woven cane.
**Weavings** – The horizontal strands of woven cane.
**Crossings** – The diagonal canes which are woven in each direction.
**Beading** – The wide cane used to create a border to cover the frame holes around the edge of the caned panel.
**Couching** – The thinner cane looped to hold the beading cane in place.
**Liner** – Centre cane or willow lining which goes around the inside of the chair frame, for knotting on to for close caning.
**Leader** – A decorative pattern or motif design which weaves into the knotted canes on the rails of a close-caned panel.
**Splice** – A patch of new cane filling a broken area on a panel of cane.
**Warp** – A textile weaving term which refers to all vertical strands, in this case all vertical canes.
**Weft** – A textile weaving term which refers to all horizontal strands, in this case all horizontal canes.
**Binding** – Describes canes wrapped tightly around a chair rail.
**Tension stick** – A piece of wood or dowel used in close caning to stop the weft canes pulling in to the caned panel too tightly.
**Steamer tool** – A flexible metal threader tool.
**Strap tool** – A flexible paper or plastic threader tool.
**Shell bodkin** – The chair caner's tool, a gently curved metal bodkin with a valley in the curved end to guide the cane.

# INDEX

First published in 2024 by
The Crowood Press Ltd
Ramsbury, Marlborough
Wiltshire SN8 2HR

**enquiries@crowood.com**
**www.crowood.com**



**British Library Cataloguing-in-Publication Data**
A catalogue record for this book is available from the British Library.

ISBN 978 0 7198 4453 9

Cover design by Sergey Tsvetkov
Cover and Contents page photographs, and Chapter opener photographs for Chapters 2 to 8 by Simon Booth



Typeset by Envisage IT
Printed and bound in India by Nutech Print Services

**DEDICATION**

For Terry and Susan South.

**ACKNOWLEDGEMENTS**

With thanks to my grandfather, Michael South – although I didn't know him, I feel connected through these skills he passed to his son, my dad, and which were then passed to me.

A special thank you to Michael Brown and Naomi South for all your support and lastly, this book is for Netty to use and enjoy!